The Doom-Laden Years

Two-year-old Alida, child of the Space Age, citizen of tomorrow, for whom this book is written.

The Doom-Laden Years

by

Alida Harvie

Regency Press (London & New York) Ltd.
125 High Holborn, London WC1V 6QA

By the same author:—

Those Glittering Years
The Rationed Years
The Sundial Years

ISBN 0 7212 0755 3

Printed and bound in Great Britain by
Buckland Press Ltd., Dover, Kent.

For ALIDA MARIA, whose coming-of-age should greet the dawn of the twenty-first century.

Author's Note

Readers' appreciation of the historical period pieces included in my books, *Those Glittering Years, The Rationed Years,* and *The Sundial Years* emboldened me to add this modest contribution *The Doom-Laden Years,* written in the form of a letter to a young relation.

The book attempts to capture the atmosphere of the twentieth century: a 'potted-history' version of the momentously action-packed social, political, constitutional and structural upheavals of the time-span 1910 to 1979.

List of Illustrations

Two-year-old Alida 2

The author aged one 8

A Knife Grinder, early in this century 10

Marie Lloyd, Edwardian favourite 13

The tragic end of the "unsinkable" British liner *Titanic* 14

Airship L287, Zeppelin 17

His Imperial Majesty the Emperor of Russia 20

Vladimir Ilyich Lenin 21

Mr David Lloyd George, 1923 23

The world-famous Charlie Chaplin 28

Lord Baden Powell with some overseas Scouts 39

President Herbert Hoover, 1928 46

H.M. Queen Mary with the future King, Edward VIII 55

Jarrow March, 1936 59

Hitler and Mussolini, 1938 62

Josef Vissarionovich Stalin 64

Mr Neville Chamberlain on his return from Germany, 1938 ... 67

Food rationing in January 1940 74

General Charles de Gaulle in London, 1940 79

St Paul's after the "Blitz", 1941 84

President Franklin D. Roosevelt 86

Field-Marshal Viscount Montgomery of Alamein 87

Mr Winston Churchill outside 10 Downing Street, 1943 ... 90

Camouflaged tank in France, 1944 91

Pre-fabs at Gretna Green 98

The Royal family at the wedding of H.R.H. Princess Elizabeth
and Lieutenant Philip Mountbatten, R.N. 101

"Teddy Boys" in 1955 108

Sir Anthony Eden and Mr Harold Macmillan 113

The "Beatles" together again 120

President John F. Kennedy 122

Mr Edward Heath 133

Sir Harold Wilson 134

Mrs Margaret Thatcher 140

All illustrations, except for the first two on this list, are reproduced by kind permission of The Hulton Picture Library.

The author aged one, in the pre-1914 "era of no return".

The delicate winter sun pierced the cold mist of a January morning. My new calendar, recently set on the wall, pointed to 1984, the terrifying year of George Orwell's Police State—the year with no guaranteed tomorrow. Returning from an engagement on the outskirts of Bournemouth I noticed sadly how the violent December gale and heavy rain had brought disorder into the countryside. Fields and woods had become tangles and tatters sodden with the litter of fallen leaves. Driving along the edge of the sea, a little later, waves foaming and furious, thundering against the shore, I was put in mind of the approaching end of this turbulent twentieth century through which so many of my generation have passed.

It was then that the idea occurred to me, my little cousin-thrice-removed, not yet two years old, to set down the story of the social and political upheavals which have taken place in our country reaching back to the date of my birth in 1910, to your birth in the 1980s. We might now be living in a different planet; and perhaps one day, far away in the future, this letter may prove to be of interest to you. You will not be under the smallest obligation to read it!

So, here is the story. King Edward the Seventh had just died when I came to join my parents and only brother in a charming Georgian house in Westminster, a year before the 1911 Coronation of King George the Fifth, known as the sailor king, and his consort, Queen Mary. Many of this new king's subjects lived in outstanding luxury, but many more endured lives of unimaginable squalor and poverty. The new monarch was soon to become face to face with the bitter struggle for Irish Home Rule and the Liberal Government's determination to reduce the power of the House of Lords. The Liberal statesman, Mr H. H. Asquith, was Prime Minister.

This was the 'tail-end' of Victorian England, carried on for a further decade by King Edward the Seventh. Great changes were already visible on the horizon. Marconi had discovered wireless, a courageous Frenchman named Louis Blèriot had flown across the English Channel from Calais to Dover in what was then known as a Flying-Machine. The significance of this remarkable feat had not passed unnoticed by the far-seeing few, now alerted to the new danger which could face mankind. The horse-less carriages, as the new-fangled motor cars were called, were rapidly replacing the buses, cabs and carriages which still clattered around horse-drawn. Electric underground trains and trams had been established.

Much of London was still lit by lamplight powered by gas, which obliged a lamplighter to traverse the streets night and morning to light or extinguish the globes, carrying a long pole.

Winter sometimes brought impenetrable fogs so thick and choking that police were issued with lanterns.

Many old customs prevailed. The knife-grinder and the cane chair-menders called their way along the pavement edge. The muffin man, shaking a dinner bell, sold his wares, balancing a tray on his head

A Knife Grinder, early in this century.

covered with a cloth. The milkman doled out milk from an urn straight into jugs, usually held by kitchen maids standing on the area steps which led to basements. Coalmen with black faces poured the contents of sacks into cellars through round holes covered with metal discs. Little boys wearing jaunty caps strapped under the chin rode red bicycles stopping to deliver telegrams.

It was not unusual for professional people with babies, like our household, to employ at least six living-in staff, including a Nanny. A young nursery maid came in daily, and the footman was assisted by a daily boot boy who cleaned knives and shoes. A chauffeur with mirror-shining boots appeared when our parents needed the car.

A hurdy-gurdy, or barrel organ entered our Westminster street from time to time, grinding out Edwardian songs and tunes.

We were pushed into the park in shallow boat-shaped perambulators— 'prams' as everyone called them, with a large back and smaller front wheel. Hoods protected us from rain, replaced by a cotton canopy in hot weather. The nannies wore grey uniforms with long sweeping skirts. The maids wore striped cotton dresses in the early part of the day, always with caps, changing later into black, with starched white aprons, frilled shoulders, pleated white caps, carrying long white streamers. We slept in wooden cots, known as drop-sided, with cane sides. The wooden high-chair could be converted into a miniature cart. Our home possessed a bath with running water, although some of our contemporaries were still bathed in a hip bath in front of the fire as running water did not reach their nursery quarters.

This was the peak time of the Suffragettes, women seeking the right to vote, imprisoned for violence and enduring forcible feeding in support of their cause.

Up to this time, the British held world wide influence. Authority was centred in the financial City of London, shared by both Houses of Parliament and sustained by the enormous strength of British sea power. But history reveals that violence was also smouldering beneath the apparently orderly life of Europe. The popular press, modern newspapers, brought into being largely by the genius of Alfred Harmsworth (later Lord Northcliffe), dropped hints of possible troubled times as a result of the formidable challenge being made by Germany. The German Emperor and King of Prussia, Kaiser Wilhelm the Second, a first cousin of King George the Fifth, an arrogant man, was said to be following a new course to seek world leadership. At a later date, evidence suggested that he had become the 'captive' of the proud German Officer corps who had pressed him to declare war. Political affairs passed largely over the heads of ordinary people. Schooling had been compulsory since the 1870s but the school leaving age was thirteen. There were many thousands who could not study newspapers. It was to be another twenty years before 'the wireless' was likely to become commonplace, and television still remained half a century in the future. Wages were very low and for many the very struggle for existence was all-absorbing.

For the more fortunate, however, the theatre provided one of the greatest pleasures. Those were the days of the great actor-Managers, Sir Herbert Beerbohm Tree and Sir George Alexander. A visit to the theatre was an occasion of romance and mystery. Patrons in boxes, stalls or dress-circle found evening dress obligatory. Men wore white waistcoats, white ties and tails, always with top hats, women wore dazzling gowns, topped with so much sparkling jewellery that it became a current joke to provide ladies with bouquets of flowers in order to be able to distinguish them from the glittering chandeliers.

The Music Hall was very popular, with the famous Marie Lloyd drawing huge audiences. The writers of the time are remembered, Sir Arthur Pinero, J. M. Barrie, George Bernard Shaw, John Galsworthy, Somerset Maugham. Outstanding actors were Charles Hawtrey, Oscar Asche, Matheson Lang, Sir Gerald du Maurier and Sir John Martin Harvey, with the Vanbrugh sisters, Marie Tempest and Mrs Patrick Campbell. A well loved husband and wife were Ellaline Terriss and Seymour Hicks. Sir Harry Lauder and George Robey were in a class of their own.

The Cinema, too, had begun to develop, but the early moving pictures were seen in a very blurred and flickery form. Money remained in gold and silver. Daylight saving had not been introduced. It was said that twilight, with the soft glow of the setting sun in summer evenings produced an exceptional charm and peace completely lacking in later years.

The glamorous London season pursued its way through Court Presentation, the private view of the Royal Academy, Royal Ascot, Henley, Goodwood, countless private invitations; and for the less well-off ragtime, foxtrots and tangos. As many have described it, the epoch of pre-1914 was a pleasure-seeking world.

On 15th April, 1912 the whole country was to shudder at the

Marie Lloyd, Edwardian favourite.

The tragic end of the "unsinkable" British liner Titanic, *April 1912.*
Drawn by a French artist.

devastating news that the British liner *Titanic*, then the largest passenger ship in the world, and held to be unsinkable, had struck an iceburg in the North Atlantic on her maiden voyage. She was later described to have lost over 1,500 lives.

Throughout the year 1913 peace was still preserved despite a number of incidents and scuffles, said to have occurred in various parts of the world. The British Foreign Secretary, Sir Edward Grey, was reported to be working unremittingly to conciliate ever increasing German nationalism, while in the spring of 1914 the threat of Ulster's opposition to Irish Home Rule had become acute. "Ulster will fight and Ulster will be right" became a noisy political parrot cry. The formidable Irish barrister, Sir Edward Carson, had established a private army of Ulster Volunteers pledged to resist Home Rule. Behind the scenes the industrious Winston Churchill was making certain that the British Fleet should be ready for war in the event of so great a catastrophe becoming a reality. He was First Lord of the Admiralty.

On 28th June, 1914 a shot rang out in a small town named Sarajevo on the frontier of the one-time Austro-Hungarian Empire. It appeared that a nineteen-year-old Bosnian student called Gavrilo Princip had assassinated the Archduke Franz Ferdinand, heir-apparent to the Austro-Hungarian throne. History later revealed that this shot was part of a campaign to break away from the Austrian-ruled provinces of Bosnia and Herzegovina in order to become associated with fellow Slavs, the Serbians. (All this area later became Yugo-Slavia.) This one shot blew the whole world to pieces resulting in the maiming or killing of some twenty million human beings. It was to change a way of life never to return.

Unwittingly, this young man had set the match to the powder keg which was to blast empires asunder.

Events then gathered speed. The Vienna Government sent an instant ultimatum to Belgrade, the capital of Serbia, in the belief that the Serbian Government had been the instigator of the murder. They made the demand that the murder should be investigated by Austria and the criminal apprehended. Serbia refused. Austria then threatened to declare war on Serbia. Unwilling to see another Slav Power overwhelmed, thus giving Austria and Germany full power in the Balkans, Russia stood behind Serbia. The French, by the terms of a previous alliance were bound to stand beside Russia. If France came in, and if Germany backed Austria-Hungary, which she had promised, the

British could not stand aside. It was a terrible prospect and the British Cabinet under Mr Asquith made frantic efforts to avoid war. There was said to be ferocious disagreement between Ministers, some maintaining that Britain must support France while others demurred.

Days of intense argument followed while the Foreign Secretary, Sir Edward Grey, begged the German Chancellory not to violate Belgian neutrality which would, in fact, bring the British into war. To the British Ambassador in Berlin the Kaiser was thought to have made the remark, "Surely the British would not think of going to war 'for a scrap of paper'?"

The march of events had now reached the end of July. On the 1st August Germany declared war on Russia. Two days later, falsely alleging that the French had attacked, she made her declaration on France. Then followed the fate-fraught step of entering Belgium after demanding free passage for German troops which had been refused. As a guarantor of Belgium neutrality, Britain could no longer delay, and on 4th August, 1914 made her choice, declaring war on Germany.

The distinguished old soldier, Field Marshal Earl Roberts, commented sourly, "The Kaiser has had this war in mind for a number of years."

As the summer harvest burgeoned in the fields, with its annual promise of golden fruitfulness, few could have foreseen the volcanic upheaval of the next four years—the devastating casualties, the savage battles with their monstrous slaughter, the tragic failure of such courageously fought campaigns, the diabolical use of poison gas, the fearful losses at sea under submarine warfare, and, for the first time in history, bombardment from the air.

At the outset, the Germans held an overwhelming advantage, a much larger better trained army, generous stores of war material and strategic railways, but against this, the Allies held command of the sea. When, in September, the British sent their well disciplined Expeditionary Force, the Germans called it "a contemptible little army!" But as winter approached and throughout the next years, the horror and suffering in the trenches on both sides was to defy description.

By 1915 both sides had established themselves in long heavily fortified lines stretching from Switzerland almost to the North Sea. Turkey's entry into the war against the Allies in November 1914 caused extreme dismay cutting off the British from Russian wheat, bought extensively in the early part of the century, and blocking Russia's door to British munitions. Thus, to open the Dardanelles seemed a life and death matter to both countries. In the spring of 1915 a landing was made of British, Australian and New Zealand troops on the Gallipoli Peninsula. It was a tragic failure. After eight months of bitterest fighting and appalling privation the troops had to be evacuated. The Turks, supremely well armed, had remained in impregnable positions. And now Italy joined hands with the Allies, warmly welcomed by Britain and France.

All through 1916 the opposing armies were locked in deadly struggle. The Empire, as it was still called, stood firmly behind the United Kingdom—Canada, Australia, New Zealand, South Africa, India, all contributed richly in men and materials. The tank had been brought into use but the autumn rains and seas of mud often meant that tanks, guns, and men were sunk helplessly in the blood-soaked battlefields. Brave men piloted the planes of the newly created Royal Flying Corps, forerunner of the Royal Air Force. Their casualties were enormous. The aeroplane was still in an early stage of development and was being used more for observation than for artillery fire. An airship, developed by Count Zeppelin before the war, an enormous sausage-shaped gas-bag supporting a compartment, had enabled the enemy to drop bombs

Airship L287, Zeppelin.

in some parts of England and France. This airship soon became extremely vulnerable, but it brought terror into the hearts of those who feared it.

German submarines were now sinking British merchant ships at an alarming rate. As the outlook became blacker with the prospect of real starvation, events had now drawn the indefatigable Welsh politician, Mr David Lloyd George, to become the country's new Prime Minister, replacing Mr Asquith, a desperate and exhausted man. A well-known journalist wrote, "It was like exchanging a stick of dynamite for a damp squib." Mr Lloyd George, now to become one of the Nation's leading statesmen, was a man of immense moral courage and unrivalled energy and vigour. As leader of the radical wing of the Liberal party he had already advocated many social reforms, and as Chancellor of the Exchequer had brought in what was known as 'The Peoples' Budget' in 1909, advocating Old-Age Pensions and National Health Insurance. A fluent Welsh speaker and a man of almost limitless imagination he was now to become a virtual dictator for the remainder of the war.

You may well be wondering what was happening on the Home Front in these terrible days. There had been many changes. Women were now playing a most active part working in munition factories and replacing men in the police force, the transport services and on the land. Gold had given way to paper currency and the King had changed the name of the Royal family to that of Windsor. As there was now a need for intensive industrial effort the Trade Unions were able to drive hard bargains and wages rose sharply. By the end of 1916 the cruel casualties in manpower resources had become so serious that the Army had formed a Women's Auxiliary Army Corps, many women crossing to France to help drive ambulances. Very large numbers of nurses were now working in France, while Voluntary Aid Detachments had enrolled to take their places. Many private homes and establishments had been opened to receive the wounded. The acute shortage of so many commodities caused increasing price rises.

Meanwhile, disorder was continuing in Ireland. Rebellion had broken out in Dublin, some rebels hoping for German aid. Many leaders were executed although one commandant called Eamonn de Valera had been spared. This rising which had taken place over Easter became known as "The Easter Rising" and was to become a legendary epic in Irish national sentiment.

British losses at sea were now becoming catastrophic, food and fuel were running very short and the nation was shocked to receive the news of strikes and rioting breaking out in Petrograd, the former city of St Petersburg. Tsar Nicholas the Second, the Russian Tsar, had been forced to abdicate. Vladimir Lenin now became the accepted leader of the militant Russian Social Democrats who were to assume the name Bolsheviks—'the majority'.

On 6th April, 1917, an event of cardinal importance took place for the despair-driven Allies, America declared war on Germany. Russia dropped out of the war and the Eastern Front ceased to exist. It was to take the U.S.A. some months to fashion her army, but there was one overwhelming help that the Americans could now render—the assistance of her fleet. At last there was a sufficient naval force available to convoy merchant ships. The 'depth-charge' had been introduced to the immense discomfort of German submarines. By slow degrees the giant destruction of shipping began to diminish.

With the signing of the peace treaty of Brest-Litovsk, Russian Bolsheviks now surrendered to the Germans, freeing the enemy to throw a great mass of additional troops against the Allies' Western Front.

Holland, Switzerland and the Scandanavian countries had contrived to remain neutral but there was great fear in Britain that, with Russia out of the war, their goods would find an easy passage to Germany. In the early months of 1918, Germany was nerving herself to make one last bid for victory. Making a fierce attack to capture the Channel ports the enemy forced the British back, almost cutting off our forces from the main French armies to the South East. Decimated and battered but with unrivalled courage the successors of the 'contemptible little army' made a firm stand—the enemy's passage to the Channel ports was barred. With a million American soldiers trained and already landing in France, Germany's power began to crumble. With the French, British and Americans relentlessly pushing forward, they were forced to retreat along their whole front. By September 1918, still desperately resisting the Canadians, the Germans knew that their hour of defeat was imminent. Bulgaria had fallen, followed swiftly by Turkey and Austria. The Kaiser abdicated. German resistance finally snapped.

The famous German Commanders Erich Ludendorff and Paul von Hindenburg informed President Woodrow Wilson of the U.S.A. of their willingness to undertake peace negotiations and to sue for an armistice. On the morning of 11th November, 1918 the armistice was

His Imperial Majesty the Emperor of Russia, Nicholas II, the last Tsar.

Vladimir Ilyich Lenin, organiser of the Russian Revolution, 1917.

signed. Relief and joy throughout the world knew no bounds— Europe's terrifying powder magazine had been extinguished at last.

In his famous book *The World Crisis*, written in his trenchant emphatic prose, Winston Churchill wrote:

"For four years Germany fought and defied the five continents of the globe by land, sea and air. The German armies upheld her tottering confederates, intervened in every theatre with success, stood everywhere on conquered territory and inflicted on their enemies more than twice the bloodshed they suffered themselves. To break their strength and science and curb their fury it was necessary to bring all the greatest nations of mankind into the field against them. Overwhelming populations, unlimited resources, measureless sacrifice, the sea blockade, could not prevail for fifty months. Small states were trampled down in the struggle; a mighty Empire was battered into unrecognizable fragments; and nearly twenty million perished or shed their blood before the sword was wrested from that terrible hand."

The war was over but overpowering difficulties now awaited the world statesmen whose task it was to plan for the future. In the last days of 1918, the whirlpool of fear and anxiety began to slow. In Britain, Parliament had been dissolved and a general election called. The franchise had been extended to all men over twenty-one, and, for the first time, to married women and to women over thirty. The Prime Minister, Lloyd George was eager to preserve national unity and the Conservatives backed him, but the Labour party decided to fight the election as an opposition. When the election results were declared some three weeks after polling day, in order to give the armed services a chance to vote, the Liberal and Conservative Coalition won a substantial majority.

The Peace Conference opened in Paris on 18th January, 1919 with the leaders of the Great Powers, President Woodrow Wilson of the U.S.A., David Lloyd George, the French Prime Minister Georges Clemenceau, and Vittorio Orlando, Prime Minister of Italy. Then followed the tortuous and diplomatic haggle to settle the terms of ultimate peace. Immense reparations were to be paid by Germany referred to as the 'bill of damages'. The Treaty of Versailles was drawn up and the 'League of Nations' founded. It was to be a rigorous, oppressive and exacting peace for Germany, no equality of armaments, no heavy weapons, the German fleet put into the hands of Britain, the bridgehead fortresses of the Rhine to be surrendered to the Allies.

After long and widespread disagreement, the wrangling Powers finally agreed, and on the 28th June, 1919, five years after the fatal shot in Sarajevo, the peace treaty was signed. Changed frontiers were soon to bring a substantial number of people under alien rule. Two new countries, Czecho-Slovakia and Yugo-Slavia came into being. Russia was said to be isolated and in total confusion.

The valiant hopes of peace were to prove illusory. In Russia the Tsar and his family had been shot. An all-Russian Congress of Soviets had given authority to the Bolsheviks to organise a Council of Peoples' Commissars. The leader, Lenin, promised Peace, Land and Bread. In July 1918, having moved the Capital from Petrograd to Moscow, Lenin brought the Soviet Constitution into existence. Civil war broke out which was to continue for three years. There was said to be unparalleled confusion. In the Far East the Japanese had landed at Vladivostok holding the railway as well as the port up to 1924. There was nationalist revolt from Latvia, Estonia, Lithuania and Finland with whom peace was eventually concluded on the basis of independence. In June 1918 a Franco-British Expeditionary Force landed at Murmansk seized

Mr David Lloyd George, 1923.

Archangel and conducted operations against the Soviet for several months. Meanwhile, famine caused peasant risings. It was to be some years before the world's governments were willing to recognise the Soviet regime. The revolutionary organizer Davidovich Trotsky, a Ukrainian Jew, whose real name was thought to be Lev Bronstein, became Commissar of War and created the Red Army.

In that summer of 1919, largely among the defeated nations, disease and famine spread. Inflation began to rise. Even among the victorious nations formidable social adjustments now had to be made. There were millions to be demobilized and resettled in civilian employment. In addition, gigantic sums of money were owed, largely to the U.S.A. At the same time, the doctrine of self-determination had been firmly fixed in the minds of Southern Irishmen, and extremist leaders now began to believe that the time had come to bring it to pass. The desire for Home Rule had been exchanged for the ultimate vision of a completely independent Ireland, emboldened by the confusion of the Great War and its chaotic aftermath.

In the meantime, a calamitous 'flu epidemic had broken out, following the signing of the Armistice in which many were to die. Victims were easily found, worn down by the heart-wrenching agony and soul-withering grief of the war years; the tension, hardship and lack of nourishing food. There was to be an unusual poignancy for convalescents, even for eight-year-olds as I was, listening to the recent war marches churned out on the London barrel organs: "Pack up your troubles in your old kit bag", "It's a long way to Tipperary", "There's a long, long trail a-winding", "Roses of Picardy", "Goodbye, Dolly, I must leave you"—and the haunting, wistful tune composed by a young musician called Ivor Novello, now a world-wide favourite "Keep the home fires burning". The war was over, but the songs lingered.

In the dawn mist of golden autumn mornings in October 1919, in a Munich Hospital, a thirty-year-old Austrian Corporal was making an excellent recovery from temporary blindness as a result of a gas attack in Flanders. Released from hospital, he joined a small political group to be known as the National Socialist German Workers' Party,* derisively shortened to 'NAZI'. With his former Hindenburg moustache now clipped back to the merest shadow, this young Corporal, Adolf Hitler,

---

*Nazional Socialistiche Deutsche Arbeiter Reichs Partei.

soon discovered his gift for open air speaking. He began to tirade against the Jews, whom he had supposed to have cold shouldered him in his earlier years as a commercial artist in Vienna. Before long, this same speaker was to turn his attention to what he regarded as the unfairness of the Treaty of Versailles. Quite unknown, he railed on. The drumbeats of future history could not be heard. Mr Churchill, however, had commented prophetically, "The dove of peace will certainly need wings of steel!"

Time flowed on. The victorious Sinn Fein representatives who had won seats in the 1918 British election campaign to sit in the Westminster parliament now refused to attend. Instead they had formed a separate Irish parliament, Dail Eireann, in Dublin, declaring Ireland to be an independent Republic. The new President of the party, Eamonn de Valera (son of a Spanish father and Irish mother, born in New York, but who grew up in Ireland), declared that the future destiny of Ireland was now to be settled by war. Irish volunteers at once turned themselves into an Irish Republican Army. Those loyal to the British, the Royal Irish Constabulary, were outnumbered and overwhelmed. Recruits from among volunteer English servicemen were sent to their aid wearing khaki jackets and dark navy policemen's trousers, as the War Office Stores did not then issue plain khaki trousers to fighting personnel. This unusual uniform gave them the name of 'The Black and Tans'.

From 1919 to 1920 De Valera had been touring America raising money for his cause. He had made clear that it was his intention to "sever the last link" which bound Ireland to Great Britain. Other extremist Irish leaders now felt that this *could* be brought to pass. The English troops, organised to crush the insurrection by whatever means, meeting terror with counter terror, moved into battle and a great number of brutalities followed. By 1920 civil war had broken out leading to terrible excesses, betrayals, tortures and murders. Nothing that the British could do seemed to meet the Irish needs. For once with inexhaustible patience, Lloyd George attempted many forms of reconcialition. At length, in yet another "Government of Ireland" Bill, the British Government established two separate Irish parliaments, one for the six counties of Ulster, and the second for the South. Ulster accepted it grudgingly, but Southern Ireland openly flouted it. A campaign of ambush, arson and secret assassination, midnight murders and other outrages took place.

Utterly sickened by the continual bloodshed and shocked by the disorder which had now degenerated into criminal looting, mindless violence and terrorism, King George the Fifth intervened. On opening the Northern parliament he appealed to "all Irishmen to stretch out the hand of forbearance and conciliation and join in introducing their country to a new era of peace, contentment and goodwill". In July 1921, a truce to hostilities was signed. De Valera was now offered complete Dominion status for Ireland. He refused, maintaining his right for complete detachment and a recognition of the whole of Ireland as a sovereign state. Then, with an apparent change of heart, he gave his consent for some of his representatives to travel to London, join the British Premier and affix their signatures to a final 'Treaty of Peace'. While remaining in the Empire, Ireland in the south, was in future to become known as the Irish Free State. Contrary to expectations further battles developed. The Irish parliament in the North decided to contract out of the Irish Free State, while remaining British, and determining Ulster's future in the new parliament known as Stormont. Their attitude enraged the republicans, who organised a new wave of terrorism, with a bitter feud raging, not only against the north but between those who were prepared to accept Dominion Status in the south and those who were not. By 1922, even the Irish had sickened of this savage anarchy and at length the civil war died down. Unfortunately, for the future, the I.R.A. bands did not disappear.

It would give you a wrong impression if I were to stress that the whole of life in the post-war world was harsh, sordid and violent. Demobilization had been speeded up and, in the crisp words of an American soldier, the services were scrambling to get back into the civilian stream. "We gotta try to get all our lives back on track and run for the sunlight," he said. Many were urgently attempting to do just that. The new Ministry of Health had been given powers to help local government housing projects with state subsidies, although the "homes fit for heroes" were not forthcoming; there were too many heroes. A boom in industry followed the war and it was to be a year or two before the Government found that slump conditions were bringing about heavy industrial unemployment.

In 1921, Mr Andrew Bonar Law, the Canadian born Scot, leader of the Conservative party, resigned because of ill health. Lloyd George continued to receive the support of the Conservatives in his Coalition Government for another year. As the Irish troubles decreased, a man named Mahatma "the great soul" Gandhi in India was now conducting a passive resistance campaign of disobedience believing that the only possible future for India was independence. Many Hindu followers regarded him as a saint. In Palestine and Egypt there was also to be a great tide of nationalism with the Arab-Jewish conflict intensifying, setting a future pattern of terrorist warfare.

The map of Europe had been completely redrawn. Austria and Hungary, now separated, were drastically reduced in size, while the boundaries of Poland and Rumania had been enlarged. Alsace Lorraine had been returned to France and the French remained in occupation of the Saar. The newly constituted free state of Danzig (later Gdansk) had become known as the 'Polish Corridor'.

The tapestry of events ran on. A great blow was delivered to Europe by the American Senate withdrawing the U.S.A. from all future responsibility towards European resettlement and again stressing America's non-membership of the League of Nations. Henry Ford of America had brought about the mass production of the family car, and the Americans were also perfecting the mass entertainment of silent motion pictures in which a 'star' system was developing. The London born Charles Chaplin had projected his extremely popular comedy-pathos in all parts of the world. U.S. commercial resourcefulness was speedily converting this mass entertainment into big business. A Los Angeles suburb named Hollywood was soon to become a world centre of film industry.

In England, particularly in London, death duties were obliging the old Victorian and Edwardian families to sell their homes. This led to a wide variety of former well-kept houses being converted into flats and offices. The insatiable demand for new houses had led to great swathes being cut into the land surrounding large towns, ribbon development it was called. Thousands upon thousands of small suburban homes were being built, soon to be followed by new Underground stations, small shopping centres, churches, recreation parks, and Picture Houses as the new Cinemas were called. Some towns began to treble in size.

The war had produced a curious new fashion among women. Possibly as a result of the tragically high number of male casualties with women now outnumbering men by many thousands, the one-time gentler sex appeared with flat-chested boyish figures, closely cropped hair and skirts rising from ankle length to knee length, although slacks had not then been seen.

The world-famous Charlie Chaplin.

Theatreland which had flourished throughout the war was now booming. The popularity of novels, too, was rising. Firms like W. H. Smith, Boots and Mudies which had copied The Times Library, Harrods and The Army and Navy Stores in encouraging lending libraries, found themselves engaging additional staff. The work of John Galsworthy, Arnold Bennett, Hugh Walpole, Jeffery Farnol, Gilbert Frankau, Somerset Maugham, Ernest Raymond, E. Phillips Oppenheim, A. E. W. Mason, P. G. Wodehouse, to name but a few, was in great demand. More serious writers such as Rudyard Kipling, G. K. Chesterton and H. G. Wells were still widely enjoyed.

The wireless, which had begun to operate in 1922, was to remain a curiosity for the great majority until the end of the decade. Enthusiasts who persevered could listen to faint programmes with earphones clamped to their heads. The popularity of the cinema was bringing new names into people's lives—Mary Pickford, Douglas Fairbanks, Gloria Swanson, Rudolph Valentino and Clara Bow. Among men, football matches were still the favourite public pleasure. Sunday remained peaceful. Sunday newspapers were finding their way into more and more homes. Public affairs were largely ignored. Some of the most influential figures in public life still remained voluntary workers, magistrates, members of County and Town Councils; while members of the House of Commons received little more than a token wage. Hospitals depended almost entirely on voluntary contributions for their continuance.

Foreign travel had become unrestricted but the traveller was now obliged to take out a British passport. Since the war there had been a great fear of aliens and their entry into the U.K. was now strictly controlled.

By the beginning of 1922, the shock was borne in on politicians that the post-war boom, expected to last for many years, was beginning to run down. Manufacturers who had invested steeply in new premises to meet the demand for goods unobtainable for so long, found themselves with their products unsold. Europe, their chief export market, still remained in turmoil. Money exchanges were chaotic. The ancient British industries of coal, cotton, engineering and shipping came to a standstill. Prices rose and the country's economy began to falter. The mine-owners, unable to sell coal, had found it necessary to make cuts in wages. This had led to a strike, the miners invoking the aid of their allies the Railwaymen and Transport workers. The refusal of a temporary offer from Lloyd George enabled the other workers, fearful for their own jobs, to withdraw their support. Left on their own the miners had acknowledged defeat, their bitter resentment smouldering on, as a legacy for the future.

Lloyd George was floundering. The terrible events in Ireland, the rumour that rich men were buying honours, an event thought to be thoroughly improper, and now what had become known as the Chanak crisis, a disagreement in Anglo-Turkish relations brought about by the victory of Mustapha Atatürk (Kemal) over the Greeks, thus endangering the allied Army of Occupation on guard over Constantinople, seemed to sap his strength.

Now the Conservatives demanded the end of the Coalition begging Bonar Law, whose health had improved, to re-enter politics and form a new Government. Lloyd George resigned. In the resulting General Election of November 1922 the Conservatives gained a clear majority of seats and Bonar Law became Prime Minister. A few months later, failing health again caused his retirement and subsequent death. Stanley Baldwin, hitherto a man not widely known, thought to draw most of his pleasures from books and from his country estate in Worcestershire, became the new Conservative Prime Minister.

Mr Baldwin, a kindly man, very English, serious-minded, conventional, with high ideals, entirely lacked Mr Lloyd George's immense vitality. He was, however, one of the first to acknowledge how much the Allies owed to the unflinching courage of the "Little Welsh wizard" as many had called the war-time Premier in the last exhausting months of the Great War.

A new Minister of Health had been introduced into Mr Baldwin's Cabinet, Mr Neville Chamberlain, who was soon to steer a number of valuable and important Local Government Acts through parliament.

Politics were soon out of the public eye, eclipsed by the wedding of the young and popular Lady Elizabeth Bowes-Lyon to the shy, modest, second son of King George the Fifth and Queen Mary. The king's eldest son, the dynamic young Prince of Wales was now at the height of his popularity with his boyish good looks, physical prowess at sport and agreeable manner. Touring round the bastions of Empire, New Zealand, Australia and Canada he had proved a sensation. In India and in the U.S.A. cheering multitudes had turned out to greet him wherever he had appeared. As the year wore on he had touched Malaya, Ceylon, Hong Kong, the Philipines, Borneo and Penang where all was triumph.

A well-known journalist wrote, "When his time comes to inherit the throne this young man will surely go down in history as one of the world's greatest monarchs." A sadly wrong forecast. Another fascinating event was also unfolding. At Thebes in Egypt, the tomb of an ancient Egyptian boy king Tutankhamun had been unearthed, packed with riches defying all description. Much excitement had been aroused by the story of the curse said to be about to fall on the tomb's discoverers. Photographs of the treasures were proving spectacular.

In Italy, there had been an unexpected rise to power of a man named Benito Mussolini, a former Socialist journalist, whose sharp agitation for revolutionary change had now assumed dictatorial powers. This new leader was soon to form an official Fascist Government. As Duce (Leader) he headed a coalition of nationalists and fascists. King Emmanuel the Third appointed him Prime Minister in order to avoid a Communist uprising, and, to a country still in a state of chaos, Mussolini's prestige soon became unassailable. Meanwhile in Munich, the young Adolf Hitler had been arrested and sentenced to a term of imprisonment after his abortive attempt to overthrow the Government of Bavaria as a prelude to a march on Berlin. This "putsch", as it was called, had disintegrated when the police had fired on Hitler's supporters. It was in this prison that the German dictator-to-be dictated his book to his faithful henchman Rudolf Hess, called "Mein Kampf"—"My Struggle", a composition later to become famous.

Perhaps this is the moment to tell you a little of what was unfolding on the other side of the Atlantic. After the signing of the Versailles Peace Treaty of June 1919, the slim, pious, Democratic American President Woodrow Wilson, who had dazzled the Parisian crowds with his vision of a new world order under a League of Nations pledged to universal peace, had sustained a stroke. Seriously handicapped he was to remain an invalid for the remainder of his life. In addition to his cruel disappointment when the American Senate rejected the Covenant of the League, there were other painful misfortunes. Returning U.S.A. soldiers, veterans as they were called, found that black citizens having moved into the industrial northern towns to carry out war work were now determined to retain their well-paid jobs, many having established their families in white neighbourhoods.

Bitter strikes erupted and in the panic a bigot army called the Ku Klux Klan was reformed to re-establish white supremacy. This army, a secret· society, had been formed originally in the mid-1800s in

Southern America to keep down the negroes in the Southern states. White-hooded antagonists reappeared carrying flaming torches. They made brutal forays against the black population followed by pitiless stabbings, lynchings and drownings with many houses burnt down. The American President, a sick shadow of his former self, could no longer handle his office in the White House and retired. In 1920 a new Republican President named Warren Harding was elected by a landslide majority. Dying three years later, he was to be followed by his Vice-President, Calvin Coolidge. These two Presidents managed to change the sour national mood and the Ku Klux Klan disappeared. When Coolidge was re-elected in 1924 for another three years, America had started to throb with a rising prosperity.

Back in England at the end of 1923, Mr Baldwin's Cabinet, having decided that "protection" would be a possible remedy for unemployment dissolved parliament in order to seek a mandate from the electorate. The result of the December General Election produced a tangle. Liberal supporters of Free Trade refused a further coalition with the Conservatives and many seats had now been gained by Labour. According to precedent, Mr Baldwin declined to rule with a combined majority of opposition parties against him and advised the King to send for Mr Ramsay MacDonald, leader of the Socialists, who had consented to become head of a minority Government.

Early in 1924, the first Labour Government came into office, but not into power.

Mr MacDonald was an eloquent Scot, a lonely man, widowed for some years, and unpopular as a result of his alleged pacifism.

Most people were now beginning to benefit from the great technological advances of the twentieth century, chiefly the aeroplane, the motor car and the cinema. As material wealth made progress civilisation advanced, but it was a tragically different picture in Germany. The exacting of savage reparations had led to a catastrophic fall in the value of the German mark, leading to profound social upheaval, and the ruination of whole areas. At length, in April 1924, the American Banker, Charles Dawes, presented a report on German economic problems to the Allied Reparations Committee, and what became known as 'The Dawes Plan' reorganized the German State Bank stabilizing the currency with a foreign loan thus enabling Germany to meet future peace treaty obligations. Meanwhile Ramsay MacDonald sought to make the League of Nations more effective by attending the League Assembly and welcoming the concessions to Germany.

As the sheen of pink and white fruit blossom scattered over the pavements of Wembley, one of London's new suburbs, King George the Fifth opened the great Empire Exhibition at Wembley, an immense arena of Empire produce, laid out as a British Empire in miniature. It was to present the exhibits of the Home Country, the Dominions and Colonies in order to give visitors a vivid picture of Britain overseas. The whole of Wembley Park, as it was then called, over 200 acres, was laid out and the Exhibition remained in being for two years. In addition to the Empire produce there were many amenities including a most popular Amusement Park and Fair. Visitors to London were drawn to see Sybil Thorndike's memorable performance in Bernard Shaw's *St Joan*. The Edgar Wallace plays were also popular, and enthusiastic playgoers flocked to see the Ben Travers farces at the Aldwych theatre, starring such actors as Tom Walls, Ralph Lynn and Robertson Hare. Dramatists like Frederick Lonsdale and Somerset Maugham drew eager audiences, and young and old queued up to see the ever-popular Gerald du Maurier, whose apparent case of acting was setting a new style. The up-and-coming brilliant young actor/dramatist Noël Coward had many admirers, as had the unique impresario C. B. Cochran, producer of glittering revues.

The portable gramophone had become very widespread, particularly among the young, grinding out tunes like "You're driving me crazy!" while the box-like ciné kodak had become an important addition to holidays.

In America, running parallel to the new prosperity, there had emerged a national underground industry as a result of the law prohibiting the manufacture, transportation and sale of alcohol. Known as gangsters, based largely in Chicago, this secret industry was to turn some of its organisers into millionaires. Finally, it became known as 'boot-legging' and was to lead to a boiling volcano of crime.

The American term 'speakeasy' signifying a night Club was never taken up in the U.K. but a small coterie of society, who were later to call themselves "The Bright Young Things" formed a brittle cult of self-indulgent dissipation, dancing into the dawn against the clamour of a saxophone and the beat of a jazz band. This generation had escaped the war. Their frantic revelry was looked upon as a sign, perhaps, of renewed vigour in the country's fortunes.

School children now received meals, and the bare-footed child of pre-war days had become a rarity. For town children the open street was still a playground. Car traffic was still so slight that children played cricket with wickets chalked on the walls and bats made of discarded firewood. Younger children squatted on pavement edges exchanging cigarette cards or rolling marbles. A patchwork quilt of chalk drawn across the road would amuse small girls in a game known as 'hopscotch'. Skipping was also indulged in until older brothers grabbed the rope to tie round lamp posts then used as swinging maypoles. Very small children were often crowded into old orange boxes under which a pair of rickety pram wheels had been attached.

The B.B.C. Children's programme, which was to bring interest into many children's lives had yet to develop. The car-owning democracy was still half a century ahead. School medical attention had become compulsory, and Council 'Evening Classes' had been introduced, thus widening the horizons of all who wished to attend.

As the midsummer sun tipped the countryside with glints of gold, it really seemed as if the hideous scars of war were beginning to fade. In politics, the recognition of Soviet Russia as the "U.S.S.R." had been achieved, and there was talk of settling the Russian debt and subsequently guaranteeing them a British loan. Many felt that unemployment could be eliminated by opening doors to the ever-expanding Russian market.

It now becomes necessary to return you to the political scene as the clouds for the Labour Prime Minister began to darken. There had been much controversy with the Trade Unions followed by a number of strikes. The Chancellor of the Exchequer, Mr Philip Snowden, proclaimed that Socialist reforms depended upon a balanced budget and a sound economy. The limitation of output caused by strikes disrupted the whole country. Quarrelling among some members of the Cabinet had broken out. Uneasiness was growing connected with the Labour Party's relations with Communism. The acting editor of a Communist newspaper called *The Workers' Weekly* had been prosecuted for inserting an article thought to be "incitement to mutiny". This article had been addressed to British troops urging them to remain on friendly terms with Communist Russians. After much agitation, the prosecution was withdrawn by the Labour Attorney-General. This led to a parliamentary vote of censure. Viewing with alarm that Conservatives and Liberals were clearly against him, Ramsay MacDonald sought the dissolution of parliament, and yet another general election was called for. During the election campaign, many newspapers published reports that the retiring Labour Government had been in close touch with Russian Communism. A few days before Polling Day, a letter was published, allegedly from a Russian writer named Zinoviev, sent to British Communist leaders, urging them to promote all possible acts of sedition to bring about revolution. Grigory Zinoviev, chairman of the Comintern, had made clear that fomenting revolution was his chief aim. Many thought that the document was a forgery but the Foreign Office treated it as genuine. The letter frightened the country and rallied opinion into voting Conservative. The new Government with Stanley Baldwin as Prime Minister, and Winston Churchill rejoining the Conservatives after twenty years as a Liberal, was to last for very nearly its full parliamentary term of five years.

Life now seemed to run along more smoothly. As the gauzy haze of autumn gave way to winter, 1924 bowed out.

Civil airlines were now becoming a commercial possibility. With the dawning of 1925 the production of civil airlines had become a source of national prestige. Imperial Airways had been established, soon to develop routes to Egypt and to European Capitals, followed later by the Persian Gulf, India and Cape Town. A small airmail service had been introduced. Five years later the British pioneer airwoman, Amy Johnson, was to fly solo in a De Havilland Gipsy Moth from Croydon to Darwin, an achievement that was to make her the heroine of her generation. She had been preceded in a courageous flight by John Alcock and Arthur Brown who had risked flying across the Atlantic in a Vickers Vimy bomber in 1919. Soon it would be the turn of the American airman, Charles Lindbergh, who was to fly from New York to Paris in a single-engined monoplane to earn the title of 'the lone eagle'. All these brave pilots had shown unprecedented feats of endurance and brilliant navigational skill.

This was also the golden age of an industrious Scot named Logie Baird who produced the first transmission of a pictorial image on a screen, a link between radio and photography. Ten years later, television had become a reality. In less than thirty years it was to become possible to receive live pictures transmitted from the surface of the moon. John Logie Baird himself did not live long enough to view this marvel. He had, however, predicted its possibility.

Trade was beginning to increase, and in London, Queen Mary had opened an attractive roof garden on the roof of a London shop overlooking Kensington Gardens. This was considered a daring novelty.

Urban centres were expanding and multiplying. Gambling on horse-racing was increasing, but football and the cinema remained the most popular activities for the majority. A gradual improvement in economic conditions seemed to be contributing to a sense of national recovery in 1925. Many Department stores and shops were booming. F. W. Woolworth, the 3d and 6d store, which had arrived from America, was immensely popular. White enamelled baths were now being mass-produced, a great boon to the housewife who was also to enjoy the invention of new kitchen gadgetry. A few years needed to pass before the refrigerator and the washing machine were to become commonplace.

The Locarno Treaty, a pact of non-aggression between France, Germany and Belgium guaranteed by Great Britain and Italy was now being worked out and was to be signed by the Foreign Secretary, Sir Austen Chamberlain, with a great flourish. Very little news escaped from Russia but the Soviet economy was thought to be ossified and drab, totally lacking in incentive. Reports of poor distribution and long queues were also current.

The Trade Unions were gaining strength and had now formed themselves into a Trades Union Congress, a gathering which was to become a very formidable pressure group.

Many new magazines were now aimed at women who were insisting on smaller families. Their emancipation had led to a completely changed appearance as well as a new social freedom, quite open indulgence to drink, tobacco and cosmetics. Noël Coward caught the mood of the middle 1920s in his satirical plays, and the writer Evelyn Waugh, depicted women's change in moral values.

Men's clothing, too, had become less conventional. The top hat had given way to a bowler hat for City wear and the very formal City attire was now only seen at weddings and funerals.

To follow the story of these long-ago days, I need to plunge you again into the political arena. The new Chancellor of the Exchequer, Mr Winston Churchill, had decided to return to the pre-1914 Gold Standard. It was hoped to restore the pound sterling to its old value. This move produced an unexpected strain on the economy hampering British exports which became over-priced in a world market of severe competition. Shipping contracts fell back sharply, drastically affecting the miners whose coal production was vital in the days before oil. With a smaller demand for coal, miners' hard-earned wages were reduced. Unlike 1921, the 'Triple Alliance' of miners, railway workers and transport workers now drew together threatening a strike which it was hoped would put pressure on the Government and force the Mine Owners to avoid cuts in wages.

At the beginning of 1926 the Miners' Federation put their case in the hands of the General Council of the T.U.C. with the cry "Not a penny off the pay, not a minute on the day!" Mr Baldwin set up a Court of Inquiry granting a subsidy until May. Shrewdly the Conservative Prime Minister gave orders for massive plans to be drawn up to counter possible strike action.

The Court of Inquiry produced long-term proposals in favour of higher pay for the miners but short-term recommendations that lower pay should be accepted temporarily in the hope of more prosperous times.

With the coming of May the subsidy was withdrawn and deadlock ensued with the miners unanimous in their rejection of the Inquiry's proposals. A strike call was issued. The T.U.C., then as anxious as the Government to avoid a General strike, put forward the suggestion of selective sympathetic strikes to force the hands of the Mine Owners. Meanwhile, their plan was undermined by printers who refused to print an editorial in the *Daily Mail* considered to be a slur on the strikers.

The *Daily Mail* had published the disputed Zinoviev letter in the general election contest of 1924 and was detested by the Trade Unions. The militants were spoiling for a fight and events ran out of control. History later revealed that Trade Union leaders had returned to 10 Downing Street very early in the morning of 3rd May, 1926, for a last talk with the Prime Minister, but the house was in total darkness. Mr Baldwin had gone to bed. Later that morning the whole nation had become involved. The strike extended to all forms of transport, heavy industries, building and printing trades, gas and electricity, and was to last for nine days.

With a mixture of good-humoured neighbourly help the country's life continued and people got to work travelling in a whole variety of unusual vehicles. Many housewives drove their husbands' cars while volunteers tackled buses and trams and University undergraduates boldly drove trains. Thousands walked. The Government's careful planning paid off and food and milk were distributed. Mr Churchill

produced a newspaper called *The British Gazette*. Mr Baldwin's even
nature and good temper fostered a mood of tolerance while the public
appreciated the carefully laid emergency plans which had come into
operation with exceptional smoothness. Public opinion was warmly
sympathetic to the miners' cause but rose against this form of coercing a
Government and paralysing the nation's life. Sir John Simon (later
Lord Simon) the famous Liberal lawyer, found records that declared the
strike illegal and, with the miners refusing to conform, the strike was
called off. The B.B.C. had kept the public informed of events, in the
absence of newspapers, and many were later to express their gratitude to
'the wireless' which had saved a number of nervous citizens from their
worst imaginings. Despite a few small spontaneous acts of violence,
good temper had prevailed, the police even playing football with
strikers. The miners' resentment, however, was to be bitter and long-
lasting. They were, in fact, to remain on strike for many months, only
returning at length, driven by despair and hunger, to even worse terms.
Resentment against the Conservative party increased over the years.

  With the lingering scent of honeysuckle and wild roses still clinging
to the hedgerows, the summer of 1926 slid into autumn. During our
summer holidays, my brother and I, together with many other young
people, attended Boy Scout and Girl Guide Camps. In this way we met
the totally underprivileged, the brilliant conception of Lord Baden
Powell, the founder. By that time I knew a little of children who lived
in vastly different circumstances. My particular school ran a mission in
Limehouse delegating pupils to take on East End children of similar
age-groups as correspondents. A young girl named Gwenllian had been
alloted to me. Gwenllian, the seventh of nine children, visited my
school, as did many of her contemporaries, every Whit Monday, when
the school acted as host. From her, I learnt the meaning of poverty. Five
children in one bed, newspapers as blankets, sparsely shared food,
ragged clothing, older brothers sharing one pair of boots, freezing
houses, rats, lice and bed bugs; the eldest daughter sacrificed to look
after the family as the mother died of consumption; the sordid
surroundings of East India Dock Road. Gwenllian pierced my juvenile
complacency sowing the early seeds of a future interest in public affairs.

  Far reaching changes were, however, already on the horizon. The
Salvation Army, founded in the Victorian era, endeavoured to bring
help and comfort to the badly housed and the great mass of underfed
and neglected children, but, better still, excellent civic authorities had

Lord Baden Powell with some overseas Scouts at the Imperial Jamboree at Olympia, 1924.

already introduced better water supply, much brighter schools, good public baths, well tended recreation grounds, free Libraries and free school meals. All the marvels of the Victorian age, steam, gas, electricity, sewing machines, photography, typewriters, the telephone, were now regarded as every day needs.

Children may well have suffered from poverty, but, in those days, they were not exposed to the greedy and selfish evils of the adult world. There were no market forces offering teenagers (a term unknown in the 1920s) enormous buying power. The deafening Juke-Box music was unknown. The horrors of glue-sniffing, child alcoholism, drug addiction, gambling, promiscuity and pornography were still more than half a century ahead.

The growth of new towns now proceeded rapidly. By the beginning of 1927 there had been a great improvement in transport facilities. New roads were being laid as a result of the great spurt in private ownership of the motor car and the motor bicycle with side car. Commerical lorries and bus services had also increased. A whole string of garages, small restaurants and shops came into existence along main roads. The advance of light industry and the growth of new housing estates were also providing new employment, particularly in the south, but in the north, the old 'smokestack' industries of engineering, shipbuilding, cotton and coal remained in sad decay. The famous Victorian Prime Minister, Benjamin Disraeli, had once declared that there were two Englands, the rich and the poor. It seemed that this situation would not be solved even as the twentieth century lurched into its final decades.

Neville Chamberlain, however, the hard-working Minister of Health, had completed his overhaul of local government measures bringing all health, insurance and pension schemes under one heading. This new measure was to form the basis of Sir William Beveridge's future 'Beveridge Report' laying the foundation for the future scheme of social insurance and national health service transferring at length into the Welfare State. Rightly it was considered a worthy achievement.

Germany had now been welcomed into the League of Nations.

In London, and in the Provinces, the theatres were flourishing. There were splendid new names, John Gielgud, Laurence Olivier, Ralph Richardson, Peggy Ashcroft, Edith Evans, Flora Robson, Peggy Wood, Mary Clare, Jack Hawkins, and the widely popular Lilian Braithwaite, Yvonne Arnaud and Gladys Cooper. Musicals had become extremely colourful. 'Sunny', 'No, No, Nanette', 'Hit the Deck', 'Rose Marie', 'The Vagabond King', 'The Desert Song', with the brilliant American negro actor and singer, Paul Robeson, drawing vast audiences to Drury Lane Theatre to hear his unique rendering of "Ole man River" in the spectacular 'Show Boat'.

Sir Nigel Playfair had taken over a small theatre in Hammersmith, called 'The Lyric' where he was reviving 'The Beggar's Opera' and other classics. A young dramatist, hitherto unknown, called John van Druten, had achieved unexpected fame in a schoolboy play named 'Young Woodley'. Noël Coward continued to enchant playgoers with his wittily diverting plays.

The new system of hire purchase had been introduced, enabling citizens, many for the first time, to acquire expensive furniture, as well as vacuum cleaners, lawn mowers, bicycles, pictures and pianos. Sport was beginning to assume a much wider dimension with professional footballers, while greyhound racing was drawing unexpectedly large and enthusiastic followers. Ice skating, too, had become popular, leading to attractive rinks swiftly constructed on the fringe of towns.

The B.B.C. advancing rapidly, was now producing symphony concerts chamber music, science talks, plays, music hall shows, political debates, dance music, and sports commentaries, all from its original site in Savoy Hill known as 2LO.

The 'Talkies' following the immense success of the silent films, were soon to assume a really important role in the nation's future.

The new moon of December 1927 was so sharp and clear one could almost have swung on its horn. By early January, however, disaster overcame Londoners when the river Thames burst its banks between Westminster and Vauxhall. The whole embankment gave way, flooding innumerable houses, with the occupants drowned in their beds. This tragedy led to a startling transformation in the Millbank area of the capital city where unhygienic derelict slums were pulled down and a new embankment completed. Open spaces were created, a new Lambeth Bridge constructed and quite handsome office accommodation and residential flats were added. King George the Fifth, recovering from a serious illness later in the year, expressed a wish to open the new Lambeth Bridge. Queen Mary had declared that the new bridge would present one of the finest riverside vistas in Europe, showing the Houses of Parliament, Westminster Abbey, the Victoria Tower Gardens, St Thomas's Hospital, the famous Savoy Hotel, with the dome of St Paul's Cathedral in the distance. The flood destroyed a strange relic of Vauxhall Bridge Road known as 'The Pest Houses' built originally in the seventeenth century to house victims who had recovered from the Great Plague, later converted into Almshouses.

In the misty climate of English politics in the late 1920s the word "Left" and "Right" had little implication. Left was a vague term denoting sympathy for the 'underdog' while Right favoured energetic independence and patriotism. As the country recovered from the strike, life for the great majority took a turn for the better. It was in this milder climate that the Church Assembly of the Church of England produced a revised prayer book. The House of Lords accepted the proposal but the Commons rejected it. The country's churchgoing since the beginning of the century had seriously declined but new 'Radio' personalities such as the vicar of St Martin-in-the-Fields, the Rev Dick Sheppard, stimulated a new interest, bringing religious services into many homes.

With self-assured stability still blooming, Mr Baldwin's Cabinet brought in the final act giving votes to women, all women, divorced, widowed, married or single, who had reached the age of twenty-one. The newspapers referred to this new law as "The Flapper Vote", the name was a relic of the Edwardian age when immature young women, too young to put their hair up, tied it back with stiff ribbon. These bows 'flapped' from side to side as their owners moved, thus the term 'flapper' came to indicate a young girl. In 1928, for the millions whose hair had been 'bobbed' or 'shingled' the term seemed absurdly out of date. Even so, universal suffrage, so bitterly fought for by an earlier generation, was warmly received.

Poverty the great social evil of former times was now being edged aside by unemployment. Relying upon international trade, much of which had not recovered from war-time disorganisation, all European Governments had failed to find a way of tackling this misfortune. Some tariffs obstructed trade, many financial policies hindered exports. Keeping prices low meant low incomes with correspondingly low purchasing power. By the end of 1928 the Great Depression was looming on the horizon but few appreciated the scale and severity of the coming crisis. As a well-known writer wrote later, "How were people to know that they were walking on a tightrope with one end about to snap? How could they foretell the catastrophic fall in prices, with nearly seventeen billion shares crumbling into nothing?"

The public still paid little heed to politics. When 1929 opened there was a desperate chill with many weeks of ice and snow and a real frenzy in the bitter East wind. A lovely spring followed and with the signing of the Briand-Kellogg pact for the renunciation of war, signed by fifteen States, Mr Baldwin decided to dissolve Parliament.

Soon the lilac-scented air had begun to shimmer in the May-time breeze. The 'Glossies', weekly publications which appeared under names like *The Tatler, The Bystander* and *The Sketch*, were filled with photographs of the enchanting little Princess Elizabeth, daughter of the Duke and Duchess of York, who had just celebrated her third birthday. Social functions saw many young women, their hair crimped and waved, pushed under cloche hats shaped like upturned flower pots. The mid-twenties' extremely short skirt was beginning to lengthen bringing in a new fashion for the evening, knee length in front with a long dipping hem falling to ankle length at the back. This was considered 'chic' but was soon declared an unbecoming style. A more serious rising generation had taken the place of the "Bright Young Things" whose 'Charleston' and 'Black Bottom' dance craze had been superseded by gentler foxtrots with titles like "Tiptoe through the Tulips" and "Spread a little Happiness".

Hatred against the Germans was now much modified. Artists and writers were visiting Berlin, said to be a decadent and depraved city. War books, or more accurately anti-war books were proliferating, and a brilliant play called "Journey's End" had been produced. The former Corporal Hitler, long since released from prison, was working ceaselessly, but, at that time, his name was barely mentioned outside Germany.

The lucky few, who were known as débutantes, queued in their smart cars awaiting Court presentation in Buckingham Palace.

Polling Day, at the end of May showed the country's electoral system working erratically. Stanley Baldwin, a humane and tolerant man, who might be regarded as vaguely right wing with his belief in individual effort, liberty and self-reliance, had polled more votes than the Labour party, but was to find his Government with twenty-eight fewer parliamentary seats. Resigning at once, the reins were taken over once again by Ramsay MacDonald whose new Government, zealous for industrial recovery, was soon to find itself badly tangled and enmeshed in public expenditure.

The worrying unemployment figures continued to rise. Ministers could not be expected to foresee that this calamitous situation would still be prevalent half a century ahead of their time, but from entirely different reasons. In the later years the shrinkage of jobs was to be caused by high technology, non-existent in 1929, when the ever-pressing need to improve manufactured products in order to survive in a competitive world, would bring about the use of computers and robots, the two great alternatives to manpower. Future historians invented a phrase for this "The inevitability of gradualism".

Only a few months after Ramsay MacDonald had resumed the Premiership, in October 1929, what became known as "The Wall Street crash" in New York burst the bubble of speculation bringing in its train the economic blizzard which was to shatter the monetary and credit system of the western world. A drying up of purchasing power resulted in catastrophe all round the world. The austere Chancellor of the Exchequer, Philip Snowden, only allowed the Government a small sum for their modest inauguration of public works, more money was now transferred into the Unemployment Insurance Fund. An Education Bill to increase the school-leaving age to fifteen was defeated by the House of Lords. The Cabinet began to fall apart in disagreements about its own policies. Retirement pensions at a much earlier age was now proposed, but this, too, was turned down. Labour drifted on. The barrel organs pounded out the song "Let the great big world keep turning" and a journalist wrote of the Government, "They are like people trying to secure a nail to a base of mercury."

While not wishing to include many personal mementos in this story of our century, little cousin, one letter from our treasured grandfather might be of interest to you, as you and I descend from his parents. I add it in at this moment as it was in the early months of 1930 that he died. When I received the letter, in my first fortnight at boarding school, I was nine years old.

"2nd October, 1919.

Beloved granddaughter,

I write to you on the dawn of my 72nd birthday when you may well be feeling lost, lonely and bewildered in your new surroundings. Remember, it is better to like what you have than to have what you like. Keep cheerful, strive to be happy, be hungry to learn, and always tuck a little compassion into your pocket, with sympathy for others. Far away in the long-distant future, when you reach the end of life's rich pattern, I hope you may be able to echo the words which are in my heart this morning 'Thank you, Lord, for a safe journey'. Time and distance will never keep my love and prayers from you. Every night make a wish on the first star, and may the angels sleep on your pillow."

This letter, now sixty-four years old, crinkled and yellowing, is among one of my most tenderly cherished records. Perhaps you, too, one day, will look back on a grandparent with enduring affection and gratitude. As my grandfather so often exhorted "Don't let anything good pass you by".

To continue with the country's story. In October 1930 there was great shock at the news that the largest airship in the world at that time, the British R-101, had crashed on a hillside near Beauvais in France on her maiden commercial flight to Egypt and India. Nearly fifty passengers and crew were tragically killed. This disaster was to lead to the abandonment of airship construction. The one exception, Germany, was to persist in the building of modern airships until May 1937, when the airship *Hindenburg* inexplicably burst into flames while approaching a mooring mast at Lakehurst, New Jersey, leading to a devastating loss of life.

The old grandeur of life seemed to be slipping away. The dread misery of unemployment in the hard-hit industrial towns was rising steeply. Privately, some members of the Government admitted that they were beginning to "hurtle down a hill in a car with no brakes".

Great efforts were being made to increase diplomatic relations with Russia but the Soviet Marxist rulers stubbornly refused to acknowledge any interest in the capitalistic western world. In India, Sir John Simon's Commission had completed its Report, but Gandhi had now embarked on a new campaign of civil disobedience. Eventually, pressed by Lord Irwin (later Lord Halifax) he consented to attend a Round Table Conference on hearing of the promise of official Dominion status. This was ultimately to result in full Indian independence. Meanwhile, the British continued to remain in Egypt, frequently hampered by sporadic demonstrations of bitter discontent. Palestine raised a much more difficult problem but the real conflict between Jews and Arabs was not due to burst into uproar until the great flood of Jewish immigrants, attempting to escape Hitler's persecution, had fled from Europe. Their arrival in Palestine was then to produce an utterly irreconcilable conflict. A new disarmament conference had been called, fiercely challenged by Winston Churchill, who was also deeply opposed to the campaign for granting eventual independence to India. He also expressed his disgust at the replacement of the historic word 'Empire' for the modern alternative of 'Commonwealth'. Regret was felt that this clever statesman was now to resign from membership of the Conservative Shadow Cabinet.

At the end of 1930, the popular Prince of Wales, still a bachelor, welcomed a second niece. Rumour circulated that he loved to visit the home of his eldest brother and pretty sister-in-law at 145 Piccadilly. A letter written to a friend contained this sentence, "I do envy Bertie and Elizabeth, so cocooned in their family life—they make it all such fun." The new Princess had received the names Margaret Rose. Both she and her elder sister were to be doted upon by their Royal grandparents.

By the beginning of 1931, politicians were stirring restlessly. The ordinary people knew little of what was going on. While some studied newspapers, only a limited few owned wireless sets, and it was to be very many years before television would become a national landscape.

In America, President Herbert Hoover, who had worked unremittingly at the beginning of the 1920s to organize the feeding of starving Europe, had replaced Calvin Coolidge. Shocked and horrified

President Herbert Hoover, 1928.

by the financial volcano which had erupted on the floor of the New York Stock Exchange in October 1929, Hoover had declared that this 'Everest' of money was a mountain of credit on a molehill of actual funds. The depression was now biting so deeply that hideous shanty towns had proliferated with men and women desperately warming their few rations over scrap-wood fires, drawing water from polluted rivers. Many had committed suicide. Others were to die of malnutrition and exposure. A poignant song had been composed "Buddy, can you spare a dime". Some recalled the words of the Old Testament 'the whirlwind by day and the darkness at noon'.

Unemployment was to become a world-wide human tragedy, but in Britain, many were fortunate enough to remain in work. The whole situation was soon to prove beyond the grasp of MacDonald's Cabinet.

The world economic crisis of the summer of 1931 was to lead straight into a British political crisis. To some the news dropped like a landmine. Expenditure on unemployment had risen so sharply that the Chancellor of the Exchequer published estimates of the balance of payment showing a considerable deficit. Having set up a Commitee of Inquiry, Parliament went into recess. When the Report showed the grave financial plight of the nation, confidence was shaken, foreigners started to sell sterling, and Bank of England reserves began to drain away. "We are on the edge of a precipice!" screamed the tabloid press.

On 24th August, Ramsay MacDonald resigned, but the King, while accepting his resignation, begged him to form a National Government which should include Stanley Baldwin, and the leading Liberal statesman, Sir Herbert Samuel. There were to be leading Labour party members, Philip Snowden, J. H. Thomas and Lord Sankey, while the Conservatives were to be joined by Neville Chamberlain, Sir Philip Cunliffe-Lister (later Lord Swinton) and Sir Samuel Hoare (later Lord Templewood). Lord Reading, the famous Liberal lawyer and former Viceroy of India, had also accepted an appointment chiefly because Lloyd George, still the Liberal party leader, was too ill to take part. Sir Herbert (the future Lord) Samuel made the statement, "This is not a coalition, it is a co-operation of individuals drawn together to push through some very harsh measures." While Conservative and Liberal parties decided to support this new National Government, the Labour party and the T.U.C. drew up a manifesto repudiating it. Parliament produced a vote of confidence and the new National Government won an overwhelming victory in the October General Election which followed. The gold standard was dropped and a whole series of financial negotiations was entered into. The parties had drawn together as they had explained to carry out whatever seemed the best remedy for the country's ills.

It was noticeable that the former Minister, thought to possess the most sensitive political fingertips, Mr Winston Churchill, had not been included.

At the end of 1931, with shining optimism, Noël Coward wrote and produced a spectacular drama called "Cavalcade" which was to draw long queues of theatre goers to Drury Lane for many months to come. Despite the depression, other theatres flourished, possibly as a form of escapism, and actors like Henry Ainley, Godfrey Tearle, and the regal personality Marie Tempest still drew crowded audiences.

There was much satisfaction that the Schneider Trophy Supermarine flying at a speed of 340 miles per hour, had now won the coveted trophy outright for Great Britain with a third successive victory.

In Italy, the Italian Duce, Benito Mussolini, was now highly acclaimed, but in Germany, the Nazi 'jackboots' were not yet ringing on the cobblestones. The name Adolf Hitler had yet to become known throughout Europe. That time was drawing nearer. Back again in 10 Downing Street, with his two sons and three daughters, but without a consort, Ramsay MacDonald continued to struggle with the complexities of an economic system too tangled for complete understanding. A gentle man, with his Scottish accent and natural charm, one would have supposed that he would have been the last politician to earn the reputation of traitor and arch-betrayer of the Labour party. Yet, such was not the case. His neighbour at No 11, Philip Snowden, who walked slowly and painfully, leaning on sticks, as a result of a long-ago traffic accident, was also to become tarred with the same brush. Mr Snowden was so much more amusing and benign than his public image would lead people to believe. A Yorkshireman, he possessed an engaging sense of humour.

Mr Churchill, now in the shadows, that great tiger for work, set about writing the life of his illustrious ancestor, the Duke of Marlborough.

Resident domestic staff were disappearing. The motor car was beginning to transform the nation's life. Populations began to show themselves ready to buy houses outside the city area and speculative builders began to run up houses within sight of green fields and woodlands. New golf courses spread out. The wireless set, as it was still called, expanded steadily. Since the 1914-1918 war, women had outnumbered men by many thousands, a great number now lived alone. For these, the little box chattering in a corner seemed to become a substitute for company. These were the great readers in the borrowing libraries. New authors were becoming popular, J. B. Priestley, Margaret Kennedy, Winifred Holtby, A. J. Cronin, Sexton Blake, Dornford Yates, and, not least, Agatha Christie, unrivalled in her inventive genius.

But it was the cinema which was now to eclipse all previous forms of entertainment. Shining new palaces were erected in towns and villages, their decor gleaming like silver fish in sunny rivers. In the intervals between performances electric organs would rise from the hidden depth of the auditorium, stabbed with coloured lights, drowning the audience in sound. Nearly all films were imported from Hollywood until about the mid-1930s when British companies began to make their mark. Life turned into a spectacle when News Reels, soon to accompany every performance, presented current events in a breathtaking, intense and dramatic form. For some audiences it was to become difficult to differentiate between actual and imaginary life. The whole population, it seemed, cushioned themselves in massive make-believe. The war-time musician, Ivor Novello, was soon to become even more famous, a whole series of glamorous romantic musicals were to come to life.

In politics, the distinguished Lord Reading, the 1st Marquis, chose to retire, while his place was taken by Sir John Simon. The House of Commons presented an unusual appearance. The National Government benches were so crowded that members spilled over to the Opposition side. The veteran pacifist, George Lansbury, leader of the diminutive Labour party, was soon to be replaced by Clement Attlee, whom no one had picked out as a potential future Prime Minister. There was deep poverty in what were known as the 'depressed areas' chiefly in the north and in Wales. Reduction in assistance because of earnings of other members of the family to be known as 'The Means Test' created interminable domestic problems and extreme bitterness which was to last for decades. But it was poverty amid plenty as the growth of new industries, almost all situated in the south, had led to a great upturn in building, even a housing boom. Cars, kitchen equipment, artificial silk, called rayon, new chemicals, and the up-and-coming radio-gramophone all helped new traders. Building Societies and Local authorities pushed forward the desire for homes and new furniture. This disparity led to political activism but rarely to open violence. It might interet you again now to know something of what was happening in America. In the terrifying poverty engulfing so much of the U.S.A. an unlikely man, a thriving country squire of substantial means, was about to arrive as redeemer. Said to be an indulged-in 'Mother's boy' privately educated, extremely rich, and married to a rich cousin, Franklin Delano Roosevelt of English-Dutch ancestry, came forward as a Democratic Presidential candidate. A man of immense courage (he had been paralyzed by poliomyelitis in his fortieth year), he was elected in the autumn of 1932, coming in like a thunderbolt, to be re-elected in 1936, 1940 and 1944, a unique record.

The new President then asked Congress for emergency power "as great as the power that would be given me if we had been invaded by a foreign foe". Congress passed the legislation creating what was to become known as the National Recovery Administration, fixing wages, prices and labour practices. Roosevelt had become a dictator, but the country recognised his benevolence as he turned his brilliant gifts to restoring the dire plight of the whole continent. Huge federal loans for public works and relief funds were authorized. Desperate unemployed were taken off the streets to build high roads and to plant a million trees, later ten million trees, while others were put to work diversifying crops, and building dams in the great river valleys. Economic and social welfare was now planned on a National scale. Then he used his great office as the spokesman of the people's needs. The American papers wrote of him, "He looks as he is, tough, stubborn, wayward, strong as a bull!" The English thought it strange that the U.S.A. did not soak up manpower in the army, navy and marine corps, but fighting was not looked upon as a profession, merely as a tiresome emergency disruption of normal life.

It was much to the credit of the British Royal family that their popularity remained stable in a world of so much sorrow and disorder. On Christmas Day, 1932, King George the Fifth made the first broadcast to all the people of the Commonwealth and Empire. "He is a plain, decent, homely and human man," wrote the Overseas press. In a few months, the world was to start declining, with the war-minded, militant and vain-glorious Nazi Dictator, Adolf Hitler, behaving with ruthless barbarity towards opponents. In January 1933 he was to reach full power as Chancellor of Germany.

The gentle purple haze of heather hung over the moors while bees and butterflies danced and dithered taking their fill of nectar, jostled by the summer breeze. House-martins were feeding their second brood, in a hurry to have the family on the wing before the autumn migration.

As might have been expected, the world disarmament Conference had failed, and in this late summer of 1933, Japanese aggression against China, in defiance of the League of Nations, was running on unchecked. To add to Europe's worries, Benito Mussolini had declared, "I do not believe in perpetual peace, it is detrimental to the character of our people. We Italians are the natural descendants of the Romans and heirs to the glory of an Empire unequalled in history. We will now become an increasingly militaristic people." As the black-shirted members of Mussolini's Fascist party roared their approval, the call of "Duce! Duce!" echoed from the stridently admiring crowds.

In England, to the horror of many, the forces of Fascism were soon to be supported by Sir Oswald Mosley, who was to found the British Union of Fascists in imitation of Mussolini's Blackshirts. Brute force soon led to flagrant brutalities not seen in Britain for generations, which shocked public opinion. After a particularly savage demonstration in East London, the Government was roused to take vigorous action, passing the Public Order Act and suppressing provocative processions and the wearing of political uniforms. In America, while full employment was not to be reached until the outbreak of another European war (which was to set all machinery in motion), President Roosevelt's New Deal had made great strides towards restoring courage and dignity to a despairing land. The overwhelming majority of the British population still remained totally disinterested in public affairs. The Glossy magazines continued to publish photographs of Royalty, racing drivers, film stars, actors, actresses, authors, sportsmen, débutantes, and many others of the talked about famous.

The pulse of life beat on while another year passed. As the sun gilded the Thames in the summer of 1934, Mr Neville Chamberlain, who had succeeded Lord Snowden (now elevated to the House of Lords), as National Government Chancellor of the Exchequer, made a more optimistic announcement. "While serious unemployment in the old industrial areas still cloud our hopeful picture," he said, "the country as a whole should soon be able to look forward to 'Great Expectations' as a replacement for 'Bleak House'!" The economic debates in Parliament stumbled on. Like so many parliamentary debates, they created much passion but little results.

Increasingly, attention now began to be diverted towards Hitler's Germany. In what had become known as 'the night of the long knives' Hitler's henchmen, at his instigation, had massacred many of their own colleagues with extreme ferocity. Jews, too, were being cruelly persecuted in many towns. At that time, it was not easy for politicians to arouse the country to the possible need of future military preparedness. The First World War with all its suffering and heartbreaking loss of life was still far too near. There still remained a strong belief in the collective security of the League of Nations, even without American support; the public were unwilling to face the remotest possibility of another war. Only one man now began to press for urgency in the consideration of rearmament but no one listened. Winston Churchill, painting, writing and brick-laying in the privacy of his beautiful Kent home, was to remain 'a voice crying in the wilderness' until it was almost too late.

Convinced that the League of Nations was no longer effective, Italy's Mussolini began to make plans for the conquering of Abyssinia, long coveted as part of an Italian Empire. Foreign correspondents warned that war-like preparations in Italy were multiplying in great profusion.

Cooking up a frontier dispute with Emperor Haile Selassie, the Italian dictator was soon to launch his forces on Addis Ababa. This heartless campaign against the weakly armed Abyssinians was now to run on for months, an easy conquest against helpless people who did not even possess one aircraft.

With the calendar moving into 1935, a cold winter stripped the branches bare and frosted grass shimmered like crushed diamonds. President Roosevelt had recognized Soviet Russia and was now shaping his own foreign policy. "The only thing we have to fear is Fear itself," he had said. In Russia, a new name was emerging, Josef Stalin. In the Russian revolution Stalin had distinguished himself defending the town Tsaritsyn, renamed Stalingrad in his honour. Now he began his policy of "Socialism in one country" through what he had termed 'The Five Year Plans'. Later, many of his erstwhile colleagues became opponents and were charged with treason. Some were imprisoned for long periods, others ruthlessly shot.

The radiant spring brought the Silver Jubilee celebrations for King George the Fifth and Queen Mary. The country's affection for the monarchy was suddenly shown by a very moving demonstration of loyalty. The King's Christmas Day broadcasts had become enormously popular. His gruff words to the widely scattered members of the Commonwealth had struck a deep chord, "I speak from my home and from my heart to all you men and women cut off by snows, the desert, or the sea—only voices out of the air can reach you." After driving through the cheering East End of London, the King exclaimed, "I had no idea that they thought like that about me, they must really like me for myself." It was said that his very strict old-fashionedness had been his strength, a man of faith, duty, tolerance, decency and truth.

With the Jubilee completed, Ramsay MacDonald, who was said to seek no decision until it was overdue, retired from the Premiership, handing over again to Stanley Baldwin. Both men were thought to be steady, old-fashioned, civilized and humane. They were no match for the harsh, brash, strident dictators on the other side of the Channel. Mr Baldwin was depicted as having a Micawber-like temperament preferring things to sort themselves out, awaiting events rather than forestalling them. The public image of Mr MacDonald was that he was too easily stampeded, but while Baldwin hated the whole apparatus of publicity, MacDonald basked in pomp and pageantry. With some courage, Baldwin had now overcome the campaign against him, set in motion by the two Press Lords, Beaverbrook and Rothermere attempting to drive him from office by their passion for Empire Free Trade. This had failed because it was soon shown that the economic system of Empire Free Trade brought no benefit to Britain but, instead, produced stronger rivals.

In later years Winston Churchill was to describe the 1930s as "the epoch of tragically lost opportunities, futile protests, and last chances never seized".

As the brilliance of the wayside flowers and burgeoning scarlet berries now pointed to the waning days, the British Foreign Secretary made a speech to the League of Nations Assembly in Geneva. "Britain," he said, "must take the lead in steady and collective resistance to all acts of unprovoked aggression." When Parliament reassembled, a few weeks later, an embargo on the supply of arms to Italy was decided upon together with exports of raw materials. Fearful of being the cause of another war, and knowing that lack of oil would become Mussolini's

'Achilles heel', Parliament refrained from adding oil to the list of forbidden goods. Neutral America refused to join these sanctions, and the French, too, expressed anxiety.

Collaboration between the two dictators, and the prospective signing of a Rome-Berlin Axis, had deeply disturbed France. In Britain, the General Election of November 1935 returned the National Government with a very comfortable majority. In France, however, the Italian situation festered, bringing an atmosphere of deep uncertainty. Now a sudden 'dénouement' between Britain and France startled the world. In early December, on his way to Switzerland, the British Foreign Secretary, Sir Samuel Hoare, consented to meet M. Pièrre Laval, the French Premier, in a private address in Paris. A settlement was proposed with the object of concluding the war based on the surrender to Italy of large portions of Abyssinia together with a measure of economic control of Abyssinia. This genuinely realistic attempt to bring about the cessation of hostilities produced so great an outcry that Hoare was compelled to resign. Laval held on, but with his reputation seriously impaired. The young Anthony Eden at once replaced Hoare, while Winston Churchill insisted, "We have told the rapacious dictators that Britain and France lack the nerve and willpower to defy them." Meanwhile, Italian brigandry continued.

With the prestige of the League of Nations shattered, there was now to be a great deterioration in hope. A journalist wrote, "The opportunity to assert the rule of law in international affairs has been lost. The British Lion opened its mouth and roared, but its teeth were missing."

Time was speeding on. In the first month of 1936, King George the Fifth died. As the funeral cortège, followed by four Royal brothers, swung into New Palace Yard on its way to lie in state in Westminster Hall, the Maltese Cross, surmounting the crown, loosened, crashing into the gutter. Many regarded this as a terrible omen. The shadow of the German swastika seemed to draw nearer.

The new king, who was to be known as Edward the Eighth, forty-one years old and a bachelor, was still widely popular and a very different character from his stern father. Throughout his youth he had swung gracefully from function to function bobbing round the globe in all the places comprising the British Empire and still marked red on the map. Endlessly, and with good humour, he had laid foundation stones, presented medals, received addresses, attended Dinner engagements, played polo, and now, at the beginning of 1936, this former Prince of

H.M. Queen Mary with the future King, Edward VIII, after attending
the Armistice Day Service of Thanksgiving at St Paul's.

Wales resented the 'old men' who were his ministers, proclaiming that he wanted to make the monarchy more adventurous. At his side, when the heralds announced his accession, stood an American lady, a Mrs Ernest Simpson, who had divorced one husband, and, as events were to show, was soon to divorce a second. The King spent much of his free time in her company, but readers of the British press had hardly learned of her existence.

In March 1936, proceeding with preparations for fresh conquests, Hitler reoccupied the demilitarized zone of the Rhineland. Despite an immense revulsion of feeling among the French he met with no opposition from either Britain or France. Dr Schacht, the financial wizard who was now handling Germany's financial and economic life with exceptional skill, supported Hitler's undisguised control enabling him to remain unchallenged. Tourism in Germany flourished, trade was increasing, and the Nazi leaders were beginning to be treated as equals by the statesmen of the West.

Two months later, the Italians captured Addis Ababa, the Abyssinian capital, forcing out the Emperor Haile Selassie who went into dignified exile in the fair city of Bath. Very soon the Rome-Berlin Axis was to be joined by Japan. Small wonder that Mr Churchill lamented, "We are letting opportunities slip through our fingers like fairy-tale gold—the days are darkening."

The confused political situation in Spain now found General Francisco Franco, Chief of the General Staff. Leading a revolt of Army Commanders prompted by resentment at the growing socialist tendencies of the Spanish Republican Government, General Franco now attempted to gain control of the whole country, a struggle which was to lead to Civil war. From July 1936 for the next three years, this conflict was to develop into an ideological battleground for Europe. Germany and Italy assisted the insurgents while Russia sent advisers and technicians to the Republicans. Very soon International Brigades made up of Communists and other Left-Wing sympathizers arrived from other countries, many from Britain, warmly supported by the Labour party. At length, with greater German-Italian assistance, and diminishing Soviet support, Franco's insurgents were victorious, with General Franco being acclaimed head of Nationalist Spain. His authority was strengthened after the 1939 war, in which he had refused to take part, by a declaration confirming that he should remain head of state pending restoration of a Spanish monarchy. The youthful Prince

Juan Carlos, grandson of King Alfonso the Thirteenth, had been nominated to succeed. This cruelly divisive Spanish Civil war had caused endless distress.

As the last month of 1936 sped towards Christmas, the British had become involved in their own personal crisis. For nearly six weeks the crisis had remained discreetly veiled and the public did not know that, in a private meeting with Mr Baldwin, the King had declared his intention of marrying Mrs Simpson. At Ipswich Assizes Mrs Simpson had secured a Decree Nisi and was therefore free to marry again at the end of six months. Eager to avoid abdication but equally determined that the King should not marry a twice-divorced subject, the Prime Minister declared, "The Monarchy cannot be reconciled with other than complete stability, continuity and respectability." The compromise of a morganatic marriage was ruled out as the Dominion Governments refused to countenance it, even if the King himself had been prepared to undertake it. Despite the many strangely assorted supporters who rallied to the King's side, the Prime Minister's skill remained masterly. The storm had broken when the Bishop of Bradford, quite unintentionally, as he himself had maintained, had made remarks at a diocesan conference about the King's need for God's grace. This statement had released an avalanche of gossip with newspaper editors taking the cue that news of the King's private life, so long concealed, could now be made public to their readers. After a number of crisis-ridden days, the Cabinet rushed through a Declaration of Abdication Act, naming the Duke of York as the new King George the Sixth. The former King Edward broadcast to the nation before going into his self-imposed exile, reiterating that he could not reign without the support of "the woman I love". He was created Duke of Windsor, marrying Mrs Simpson seven months later. The new King and Queen, with their two young daughters, at once took up the familiar pattern of the nation's monarchy and the throne remained unimpaired. King George the Sixth, frail and inexperienced, sustained by his charming consort the new Queen Elizabeth, was to follow his father's dutiful and strict example with complete devotion, giving unquestioning support to his ministers and setting an extremely high standard. *The Times'* leader-writer wrote, "Mr Baldwin has no comparable rival in the handling of a great national problem, he gives the Cromwellian impression that he has voiced the nation's conscience."

With the brilliant autumn colours a glowing memory, and the black lace-like tracery of winter branches glistening with an early snow-fall, the last days of 1936 slipped away.

Behind the scenes, in his own private study, with the courage and dedication of a man trying to bottle lightning, Mr Churchill was talking to scientists. In his book *The Second World War* he was to write later, "The end of 1936 at last saw the slow beginning of British rearmament. A few scientists were about to change the face of history. Mr Watson Watt and Sir Henry Tizard were to develop 'radar', a device by which radio instruments would be able to detect objects in the air, thus the strategy of aerial warfare was to become revolutionized."

Meanwhile, if the cocktail-shaking, charleston-crazy mass idiocy and wild frivolity had vanished, we of the 1930s generation were dancing to the cheerful tune appropriated by President Roosevelt to add impetus to his New Deal. The words ran something like this:

> Happy days are here again,
> The Skies above are clear again
> Let's sing a song of cheer again,
> Happy days are here again.
> Altogether shout it now
> There's no one here can doubt it now
> Let's tell the world about it now
> Happy days are here again.

At the same time the hunger marchers from Jarrow were progressing through the country, in tattered clothing, cardboard stuffed into their patched boots, displaying dignified courage. A paradox indeed! But as one of the Labour leaders, rather wiser than the rest, had remarked, "You have to play the ball where it lies!" While sympathizing with the out of work, the public were turning their attention to the lavish decorations, flagpoles and scaffolding, barricades and gilt crowns, heralding the oncoming ceremony for the coronation of a new King and Queen.

From Government Offices to suburban households, union jacks, waving banners and coloured trappings flapped in the breeze. Floral decorations had turned normally grey old London and many other cities into a cheerful vivid scene. May 12th saw the coronation of King George the Sixth and Queen Elizabeth, with a floodlit illuminated Buckingham Palace besieged by enthusiastic crowds clamorously

Jarrow March, 1936.

cheering. Not even an exceptionally wet evening could damp their
ardour while all over the country, picnics and pavement parties were
taking place. Edward the Eighth had faded. Immediately after the
coronation ceremony, the Prime Minister, now a Knight of the Garter
and Earl Baldwin departed from the political contest. He was to be
succeeded by the efficient, hard-working, conscientious Neville
Chamberlain, a kindly man but unglamorous Prime Minister, whose
misfortune it was to come up against the intractable European dictators.
Ramsay MacDonald, thought to be a sick man, also retired from the
political scene. A few months later he had died.

Once again there was trouble in Ireland. Eamonn de Valera, still not
content with the agreement for 'Eire' to be totally independent from
Great Britain, wanted nothing less than the full re-unification of the
whole Irish state. The Unionist Government of Northern Ireland
rejected· this proposal with furiously emphatic vigour. This intense
grievance and bitter quarrel between people of the same community
was to break out again in thirty years. As Lloyd George had once

stated, "Nothing will satisfy the Irish, it matters not what well-meaning British politicians try to do, centuries of history have divided them."
The partition of Palestine under an Arab state and a Jewish state was beginning to look equally insoluble.
The British public, however, paid little heed. Queueing up in their thousands they watched the News Reels of the Coronation procession in places called Plaza, Gaumont, Odeon, Granada, Ritz, Empire and A.B.C.—sometimes Mayfair, Paramount or Curzon. Many thousands now owned their own homes and hire purchase had brought hitherto undreamed of luxuries within their reach. Millions of households now possessed a wireless set, while a small number had been able to procure some of the early television sets. The B.B.C. had started a small television service with regular transmissions from Alexandra Palace.
As autumn 1937 approached, the Lake in St James's park looked like rippling quicksilver. Behind the misted opal flower-beds and tang of bonfire smoke, the façade of Whitehall concealed a hive of activity—the development of increasing technology, pressed so urgently by Mr Churchill, was galloping along. History later disclosed that, at this time, Germany was only busy in preparing to become a military power in the old continental fashion, her efforts aimed at the creation of a force for land operations. It transpired that she was not making preparations for any war against England. She had no battle fleet, no landing craft and very few submarines. Her Air Force was designed for co-operation with the army, not for use as an independent weapon. Sir John Simon, who had now become Chancellor of the Exchequer, called finance "the fourth arm of Defence".
There were many in the country who regarded the making of armaments as the cause of war, hence the enormous list of signatories of the "Peace Pledge Union". The new Prime Minister resented the money now to be spent on armaments. Foreign affairs distracted him pulling him away from his enthusiastic projects of domestic reform. He still believed in Great Britain's former shield of widespread sea power.
While there was concern about events in Europe, it would be a mistake to leave you with the impression that politics remained high in the nation's interest, or that the tragedy of unemployment played more than a minor role. In the 1930s people lent themselves to hobbies and activities of every kind. To list but a few, there were the Royal Agricultural Shows, Boxing, Yacht Racing, Rock climbing, Meets and

Point-to-Points, Tennis, Cricket, Golf, Rowing, Car Racing, Morris Dancing, Fairs and Circuses, to say nothing of the Brass Bands of the Trade Union Brotherhood. In addition, constant queues gathered for Ivor Novello's romantic musicals, 'Glamorous Night', 'Careless Rapture' and 'Crest of the Wave'. In Regents Park the newly established 'Open Air Theartre' was tempting audiences to see 'The Merry Wives of Windsor', jestingly called 'The Merry Wives of Saxe Coburg & Gotha' after the caustic comment made by Kaiser Wilhelm when his cousin, King George the Fifth changed the Royal title.

Inside Buckingham Palace, the twelve-year-old Princess, christened Elizabeth Alexandra Mary but called 'Lilibet' in her private world, was making new friends among members of her Girl Guide Company. The annual summer camps, established by the King when Duke of York were still very popular.

Opera and concerts, the Proms, the Chelsea Flower Show, the Aldershot Tattoo, the Royal Naval Review, and the Royal Air Force Pageant at Hendon were never without their enthusiastic supporters.

The Derby, Wimbledon, the Henley Royal Regatta, and the famous Olympic Games, held in 1936 in Germany, also drew their own admiring gatherings.

In the world of the cinema many names were now 'star quality' Greta Garbo, Joan Crawford, Bette Davies, Clarke Gable, Spencer Tracy, Cary Grant and a great number more. There was no inflation and enjoyment was within the reach of many thousands.

1938 dawned with thin slithers of ice covering lakes and ponds, a white snow carpet, and a withering frost. It was at this point that President Roosevelt put forward the idea of a World Conference with the object of clearing the air of so many of the world's grievances. The Prime Minister, Mr Chamberlain, stalled, awaiting the return of Lord Halifax who was in the process of undertaking a private discussion with the German Chancellor, Hitler, about the future of Danzig (not yet called Gdansk) and the area known as the Polish Corridor. He was also to discuss with Hitler the future of Austria, and the problem of the Sudeten Germans in Czechoslovakia. Piqued that, as Foreign Secretary, he had not been consulted, Mr Anthony Eden made a vigorous speech declaring that a great opportunity had been missed.

A month later, Mussolini demanded recognition of his new Empire in Abyssinia. Pressed by his desire to propitiate the Italian dictator and scared by Germany's ever increasing military power, the Premier gave

Hitler and Mussolini, 1938, a "Dictators" meeting.

way. In disgust Anthony Eden resigned. His post was immediately filled by Lord Halifax.

Noting Mr Chamberlain's sign of appeasement towards Mussolini, Hitler was to make fresh plans.

On 12th March, assuming supreme command of all the armed forces of the Reich, German troops marched into Austria with Hitler at their head, occupying Vienna and moving on to the Italian frontier at the Brenner Pass. Hitler, an Austrian by birth, displayed much emotion making a speech on the outskirts of Linz, his birthplace.

In the House of Commons Mr Churchill spoke gravely. "The frontier of Czechoslovakia now lies exposed to future German advance," he said, "we are confronted with a programme of aggression carefully calculated and timed stage by stage." His words were soon seen to be prophetic when German troops began holding military manoeuvres on a grand scale along this new border.

Mr Chamberlain calling together the Chiefs of Staff made the sour comment, "To take offensive against Germany now would be like a man attacking a tiger before he has loaded his gun."

A little later he made a statement in Parliament, "You have only to look at the map to see that nothing that France or Britain could do could possibly save Czechoslovakia from being overrun by the Germans if this is what Herr Hitler is determined to do. I have therefore abandoned any idea of giving guarantees to Czechoslovakia." Private friends reported a further statement made by Chamberlain, "If France should become involved in war for the defence of the Czechs, then the inexorable pressure on us might prove stronger than formal pronouncements."

Hitler paid no attention, continuing to stage an elaborate parade of indignation about the wholly alleged ill-treatment of German citizens in the Sudetenland.

As the unveiling of Hitler's plans became more menacing Chamberlain sent Lord Runciman to Prague to act as conciliator and adviser. The Prime Minister still believed that the German and Italian Dictators were rational statesmen and that their difficulties could be eased and their discontents sorted by rational discussion. Critics were beaten down with the question "What is the alternative?" And indeed, no one now believed in the League of Nations.

Throughout these months, the unknown Soviet Russia was in the middle of Stalin's cruel purges. It was assumed that Russia still wanted to communize Europe. If Russia remained an enigma, there were many

Josef Vissarionovich Stalin.

who felt sympathy with Hitler, agreeing that the Treaty of Versailles had been unjust, too punitive and barbaric. As the French statesman, Georges Clemenceau had queried, "Are we being too harsh?" "Are we laying up trouble for new generations?"

Spring advanced with the glow of a lemon-yellow sun. While birds were busy building their nests for a new season, bees attacked the nectared sweetness of spring flowers and early butterflies seemed to be romping in sunbeams. All around a new pulse of life throbbed on. Even if the news cast a dark shadow, black with peril, holidaymakers made plans to follow their individual pleasures, fishing, gardening, bicycling, hiking, sailing, bird-watching, photography, or whatever pursuit they preferred.

By the end of August the Prime Minister admitted to a friend that he felt like a man walking on a razor blade. Chamberlain still believed that quiet discussion could bring Hitler back to civilized behaviour. The Labour party continued to stress the necessity of collective security even if unsupported by arms. Anthoney Eden, the former Foreign Secretary, still a power in Parliament, relied on strong words of condemnation but no acts. President Roosevelt had made clear that, beyond talks, the United States did not intend to move in any way. France displayed impotent disapproval.

In early September the British Government began to think of ways to extract concessions from the Czech Government about the three million German subjects who resided within Czech borders hoping to reach a solution before Hitler moved in by force. Hitler's sole object was to discredit the Czechs in the eyes of the Western Powers. Convinced that the British and French would not move against him, he did, however, fear Churchill, the man who had constantly sounded an alarm.

On 4th September a crisis exploded. Beñes, the Czech head of State, agreed to all the demands the Czech-Germans had made, but this was not enough to suit Hitler's plans. Led by agitators the Czech-Germans were forced to revolt, but order was soon restored. Hitler's threats became more menacing.

The desperate French Cabinet appealed to the British Prime Minister, "The entry of German troops into Czechoslovakia must be prevented at all costs, all possible moral force must be used."

It was later reported that Chamberlain himself did not regard the question of Czechoslovakia as a British interest, he did, however, feel that his intervention was now imperative if he was to avert a second

European war. Accordingly, on 15th September he flew to Munich travelling with Hitler who had greeted him to the German Chancellor's private retreat at Berchtesgaden. The Munich crowds greeted the elderly British statesman with rapture, he was in his seventieth year. His city suit, black homburg hat, and rolled umbrella, contrasted strangely with his host and the many surrounding henchmen all wearing immaculate Nazi uniforms. Talks were entered into, the British Premier attempting to seek a peaceful solution by mediation, even if mediation meant the immoral suggestion of separating the Sudeten Germans from Czechoslovakia.

In Paris, the nerve of the apprehensive French Government began to falter, M. Daladier and M. Bonnet flew to London. Daladier argued that Hitler's real aim was to dominate Europe. "If we agree to guarantee this truncated Czechoslovakia, will the British guarantee France?" was the French statesman's query. The British Cabinet was forced to agree. When the ultimatum was sent to President Beñes, he regarded it as a grave betrayal and resigned from office. On 22nd September, returning to meet Hitler at Godesberg, expecting only to discuss terms, and settle details, Chamberlain was horrified to find that Hitler had increased his demands. Not satisfied with the transference of territory, he wanted immediate occupation. Appalled, Chamberlain appealed to Mussolini who agreed to step in. On 29th September, after a most dramatic scene in the House of Commons, Chamberlain, Daladier, Mussolini and Hitler met again in Bad Godesberg and agreed terms. In Berlin Hitler declared violently, "This is the last territorial claim I shall make in Europe."

Chamberlain flew back to London to be welcomed with immense enthusiasm as the man whose initiative had saved the world from a second European war. The new Czech Government rejected the demands and called for immediate mobilization. Behind the scenes the French and British were also calling up Reservists. The initial hysterical relief of people who had been digging trenches and trying on gas masks soon gave way to a mood of shame. "Hitler has broken even his own promises," commented a sombre Mr Churchill, "he has openly tricked the Prime Minister and we have taken part in a cruel betrayal."

The general public, however, returned to normal life with grateful relief. The theatres, almost empty, picked up rapidly. The Musical Comedy "Me and my Girl" then playing at the old Victoria Palace set a

Mr Neville Chamberlain on his return from Germany—'Peace In Our Time', 1938.

new trend in dance patterns, 'The Lambeth Walk' it was called. Its popularity spread across the land. At the same time, the Czechs were deprived of their fortifications while half a million Czechs, together with three million Sudeten Germans, were incorporated into the German Reich. "A total and unmitigated defeat," growled Mr Churchill. Many thoughtful citizens were shocked at collective 'blackmail' and opinion quickly hardened in favour of immediate rearmament. The British Cabinet did not stand still, Sir John Anderson, a brilliant organiser, was called in to direct Civil Defence preparations such as the evacuation of children from city areas, air raid shelters, emergency fire, ambulance, and transport services, together with many schemes for the assistance of voluntary organisations such as the Salvation Army and the Women's Voluntary Service. Chamberlain had at least bought time.

As November 1938 opened, the mother o'pearl streaks lighting up a slate-grey sky displayed a whole series of ambulances marked A.R.P., Air Raid Precautions, being driven by youthful volunteers. Unspoken fear still hung in the air before the world moved into the fateful year of 1939.

The dreadful crisis-ridden summer of 1938 had not been all gloom. One extremely happy event had taken place in Paris which I am sure you would like me to record. It concerned the official State visit of King George the Sixth and Queen Elizabeth to the French capital. British Queens had conquered before, particularly the radiant Queen Alexandra in 1907 when her beauty and her clothes were said to have cemented the Entente Cordiale, but Queen Elizabeth was to receive a welcome of such unrestrained delight that photographs of her exquisite dresses, her simple dignity and sunshine smile were in demand all over the world. Just before the Royal pair were due to leave England, it happened that the Queen's mother, Lady Strathmore, had died. This threw the Royal dressmaker into a dilemma. Obviously the designer could not pass a collection of coloured clothes, so white was decided upon. Revellers, who had been grim with worry over the possibility of coming war, stayed in the streets to cheer as the Queen accompanied by her devoted husband, the King, visited the Elysée Palace and the gardens of the Quai d'Orsay. The distinquished Norman Hartnell, who had transformed Her Majesty's outfits into white, later gave a newspaper interview from which I quote: "Her Majesty the Queen never looked so beautiful. For the Elysée Palace she wore a white bodice and billowing skirt composed of hundreds of yards of perfect Valenciennes lace sprinkled with silver. For the Gala Opera we had given her a spreading gown of thick white satin, held by clusters of white camelias. Her dress at the Garden Party at Bagatelle was made of the finest cobweb lace and tulle, worn with a sweeping hat of white osprey borders. Her parasol against the sparkling sun on the lakeside of Ile Enchanté made of transparent lace delighted all onlookers. For the luncheon held in the Galeries des Glaces at the Palace of Versailles, the Queen appeared in a glorious spreading dress of white organdie embroidered all over in openwork design of broderie anglaise. Her becoming hat had been trimmed with dense black velvet."

Life was to be torn out of the world before any future Royal visit could send a Queen with outfits so ravishing.

Hitler did not waste the next months. Germany had now gained immensely in strategic advantages. She had destroyed the thirty-six Czech divisions and acquired the famous Skoda works and many other resources. Few now trusted Hitler, although Chamberlain made the statement in Parliament, "I believe Europe is now settling down to a period of tranquility." Churchill remarked privately to friends, "Information has reached me that Germany is mounting forces to menace Poland." The Service chiefs, much disturbed, were looking on war as more or less inevitable. Government critics had begun to clamour that Churchill and Eden should be brought back into the Cabinet. Chamberlain resisted these demands on the grounds that Cabinet changes might increase tension in Europe. The Prime Minister, Mr Chamberlain, and Lord Halifax, who had made a secret visit to Mussolini, had returned convinced that Mussolini would be able to exercise a moderating influence on Hitler. A few days later, the British Government was to recognize General Francisco Franco as the rightful ruler of Spain.

On 10th March, to the surprise of many, Sir Samuel Hoare made a speech to his Chelsea constituents telling them that a Golden Age was approaching and that as soon as British rearmament had been completed, leading to full co-operation between the Great European Powers, Russia included, there would be a raising of living standards never before envisaged in the twentieth century.

These cold, blustery days of March 1939 may well have counted as 'the lull before the storm'. At a later date, Ernest Bevin gave this verdict, "If you want to ask me who was really responsible for the outbreak of war, I would say, 'All of us'; we absolutely refused to face the facts." Only Churchill confronted reality.

On 15th March, 1939, the desperately weakened state of Czechoslovakia fell to pieces becoming a German protectorate. The Army and Military Police moved in, establishing the same NAZI dictatorship as in Germany. Hitler made a visit to Prague.

"Nothing will stop him now," thundered Mr Churchill, "here is clear proof of planned aggression, he is on the march to world domination." Others supported Churchill in a 'firm front of resistance' but the Prime Minister snapped "Great Britain has nothing to gain by war" while Sir John Simon explained that it was impossible to fulfil a guarantee to a state which had ceased to exist. To the majority of the Cabinet, war still seemed an unmitigated disaster. There were now rumours of German troop movements against Poland.

At the end of March, Chamberlain sent an assurance to the Poles that, if their independence were threatened, Britain and France would at once lend them all the support in their power. As one of the Chiefs of Staff commented, "How do we put teeth into an alliance with Poland?

We have no teeth for such an undertaking." Hitler withdrew into silence. The advocates of a strong line made the false assumption "The British lion has roared and Hitler has been hit on the head!" Churchill continued to press for the establishment of a Ministry of Supply, and for consideration of compulsory military service. The Opposition however, resisted these moves. Churchill replied fiercely, "Having begun to create a grand alliance against aggression we cannot afford to fail, we shall put ourselves in mortal danger." The veteran war-time leader of an earlier war, Mr Lloyd George, spoke up even more emphatically, "If we go to the help of Poland without seeking help from Russia we shall be putting our heads straight into a trap." The Prime Minister expressed his scepticism. Privately he asserted, "I must confess to the most profound distrust of Russia. I have no belief in her ability to maintain an effective offensive, and I distrust her motives. But it is desirable not to estrange Russia." Soviet policy remained in total obscurity.

Through these painful weeks, the King and Queen were away on a seven-week tour of Canada and the United States. The invitation had come from Mr Mackenzie King, Prime Minister of Canada, and, on hearing that it had been accepted, President Roosevelt suggested that the journey should be extended to include Washington, New York, and a weekend at his country home. The Royal couple had embarked on the Canadian Pacific liner *Empress of Australia*. Travelling with the party was a young British woman journalist whose letters to my mother were quite revealing.

"We ran into icebergs and fog," ran the description, "the Captain never left the bridge. It was frightening that we could no longer see our escorting cruisers *Southampton* and *Glasgow*. Our sirens blared for two days, a most mournful sound. However, a pet canary, thought to be male, had laid an egg, and this was looked upon as a good omen. The melancholy siren blasts seemed to be echoed back by icebergs, like pulling your harp strings! Making a kind of twang. At length the weather cleared and we seemed to be rushing full speed up the St Lawrence river. The shore was alive with car headlights and flickering bonfires. At our first luncheon the King spoke so well he quite overcame his speech impediment. He even dived under the table to retrieve a lady's lost handbag! The Queen, of course, captured all hearts. Her 'hostess dress' in her favourite powder blue was so much admired. The journey in the Canadian Pacific Railroad track defies description—coaches all air conditioned and fitted with radio and telephones—the food was lavish. There was a hairdresser, a barber and even a post office. The log cabins flew Union Jacks and the initials 'G' and 'E' had been spelled out in stones. Wherever they went there was a great roar of welcome. Their contact with the crowds was amazing, the crowds swallowed them and the Scotland Yard bodyguard were horrified. The American Press were staggered, one man saying to me, 'No U.S.A. President would ever dare to go right into a crowd with no protection at all.' Some of the mêlées were enormous."

The letter continues with the King and Queen entering America. "They were met by Mr Cordell Hull, Secretary of State, who presented the Queen with a sensational bouquet of orchids. To the King he said, 'Your Majesty you are the first reigning British sovereign to enter the United States. When you meet the President it may be the most important handclasp of modern times.' Later, as at home, the King was addressed only as 'Sir'. There was lunch at The White House, and WHAT an impressive place it is! One Roosevelt grandchild called the Queen 'The Fairyqueen' while later a faithful negro servant referred to her as 'she's jus perfec that honeychile Mrs Queen!' I didn't hear this but one of the senators repeated it. The Royal Pair entertained the President and Mrs R at the British Embassy. The President's wife is kindness itself but she is not handsome; she and the Queen talked a great deal. The table groaned with silver but nothing could outshine the Queen in a frock of rose tulle with a magnificent diamond tiara and diamond necklace. In New York, the ticker tape tumbled down—the New Yorkers are certainly very friendly people. The President is amazingly brave. He is such a wonderful conversationalist and shows no sign of his discomfort, evidently he is quite helpless and must often feel pain. He and the King are reported to have talked late into the night discussing international affairs."—Here the letter ends.

Naturally the writer was not included in the King and Queen's private visit to Hyde Park, the Roosevelt ancestral home, but the Queen's dresser gave her this story. "Mrs Sarah Delano Roosevelt then eighty-five years old, the President's masterful mother, had insisted on offering tea to the Royal visitors. 'My mother doesn't approve of cocktails,' stressed the President. 'Neither does mine,' the King is reported to have joked in a smiling reply."

Bearing in mind the approaching war in Europe now considered to be unavoidable, this visit must certainly have forged a vital link between

between the Old World and, as Churchill was soon to call it "The New World across the sea".

The weeks ran on. By late August the hedgerows were ablaze with berries, shimmering with the early morning gossamer of spiders' webs. The staunch Stalinist supporter, Vyacheslav Molotov, Soviet Russian Commissar for Foreign Affairs, had suggested military talks between Russia, Britain and France. The Soviet leader Voroshilov at once raised the point "How can the Red Army make contact with the enemy without violating Poland?" The talks ran into the ground. The British Government, having failed to secure an alliance with Russia, also failed to convince Hitler that any violation of Poland would be resisted. It was said later that Hitler had assumed that a speedy attack on Poland, a blitzkrieg (lightning war), could be carried out without involving Britain and France.

The British Government, now at a loss, drifted on, while Hitler remained silent, and tension mounted in Danzig. News then broke that Joachim Von Ribbentrop, the German Foreign Minister, had been invited to Moscow. On 23rd August he and Molotov signed a Nazi-Soviet pact with Russia promising to remain neutral should Germany become involved in war. Like the British, the French did not know what to do and stood aside. The reaction of British public opinion was bitter, but there were no marches, no demonstrations, no public meetings. Members of the House of Commons expressing deep dismay suddenly became resolute. Parliament was recalled passing an Emergency Powers Act through all its stages. On 25th August the Anglo-Polish treaty of mutual assistance was at last signed. Secretly the Prime Minister implored President Roosevelt to put pressure on the Poles to hand over Danzig. This approach failed because Joseph Kennedy, American Ambassador in London, informed the President that no one could save the Poles and that the British would have no chance of victory should war develop.

Hitler now responded demanding that the Polish plenipotentiary should come to Berlin to discuss German terms for a settlement. The Poles refused. On 1st September, 1939 German troops crossed the Polish frontier and aircraft bombed Warsaw.

For the British, this was not quite the end. Sir Nevile Henderson, the British Ambassador in Berlin, who had worked incessantly to try and bring the Poles to undertake one last negotiation with Hitler, was recalled to London. He conveyed the news that Mussolini appeared to be on the point of proposing a conference. The French statesman, M. Bonnet, was said to be eagerly seconding the idea, partly to give the French Generals more time, desperately needed if full mobilization was to be carried out. The British Cabinet, however, insisted that all German troops must be withdrawn from Poland before any conference could be called. Lord Halifax urged that a conference could still be held even without a time limit attached for the withdrawal of troops. In Parliament there was utter confusion. Ministers met in Sir John Simon's room carrying the message to the Prime Minister, "Ultimatum cannot be delayed, war *must* be declared." Churchill used stronger words, "Every minute's delay is imperilling the very foundation of our national honour." One more day passed. Then the British ultimatum was delivered to the German Government at 9.00 a.m. on 3rd September, 1939. There was no reply. A few hours later the deeply reluctant French Government also declared war on their old enemy, Germany. Within a very short period the Empire had followed. Eire remained neutral.

Listening to the heartbroken voice of the Prime Minister, the British people accepted the situation uncomplainingly. It had long been expected. Not for the first time in their history the British rose united. This dictator's ruthless ambition to dominate the world HAD to be checked expressed in faulty grammar! In London, in the cool and beautiful September light, over the roofs and spires, a mass of gleaming cylindrical balloons were rising.

Once again life became totally changed. In the countryside, where many children were soon to be evacuated, blackberries shone like polished shoes, and horse chestnut leaves turned a dazzling yellow. Everything was to remain uncannily quiet for the first six months. It was to be nearly a year before the ruin and carnage we all feared was to arrive, with explosions shaking the ground. Then buildings would come clattering down in dust and ruin with fire brigades and ambulance crews hastening through the smoke and fire. The terrifying future drone of hostile aircraft had yet to be experienced. Mortal peril was to threaten the whole nation before another autumn had turned the oaks bronze.

Meanwhile, Hitler needed all his aircraft for his brutal campaign against the Poles. It was possible that he hoped that the British and French would call off their campaign once it become obvious that Poland had been conquered. In the meantime the R.A.F. were sent off to drop propaganda leaflets over Germany. They were difficult days. Street lighting had been extinguished, cars drove with the merest slits of headlights, all windows were concealed with black-out curtains, and to begin with, theatres, cinemas and schools were closed. Sandbags protected shop windows with notices 'We are open' dangling on lengths of string. Food ration books were not used until early 1940 when the admirable Lord Woolton was appointed Minister of Food. Military conscription for men extended from 18-41. Conscription for women did not become law for another two years. At the beginning, Land Girls and Factory workers were more urgently needed.

There was great rejoicing when Winston Churchill returned to the war Cabinet taking up his old post as First Lord of the Admiralty.

As in the First World War, an expeditionary force had been sent to France consisting of four divisions. It was said that the Chiefs of Staff were running three wars.

In Italy, Mussolini had announced his non-belligerence while the French army remained safely garrisoned behind their Maginot Line.

Food rationing in January 1940 with the issue of ration books.

The King and Queen remained at Buckingham Palace with their young daughters, but Queen Mary had been prevailed upon to move to the Duke of Beaufort's house at Badminton. Anthony Eden was brought back into the Cabinet as Dominions Secretary. A number who were still in a position to do so began to emigrate to America. Most ordinary citizens, cardboard boxes containing Government-issued gas-masks dangling from their arms, carried on as best they could with their ordinary affairs. Information was now received that the British Expeditionary Force had thrown up a few defences on the unprotected Belgian border. Troops sang a derisive anti-German song 'Hanging out the washing of the Siegfried Line' or another entitled 'Lili Marlene'.

General Sir Archibald Wavell was placed in command of the Middle East. General Gort controlled the forces in France.

While the German U-boats were still small in number, they had sunk the aircraft carrier *Courageous* and the battleship *Royal Oak* causing extreme dismay. There was better news in December when British ships forced the pocket battleship *Graf Spee* to seek refuge in Montevideo where, on Hitler's orders, she scuttled herself, but not until there had been heavy losses of cargo ships. The German invention known as the magnetic mine was overcome by a system called degaussing, a strip of wire running round the hulls.

Ordinary life continued with many war weddings, black-out accidents, and sporting events not yet eclipsed. Theatres and cinemas had been reopened.

As Christmas approached, it became known that hundreds of evacuated children had returned to their city homes. Great efforts were made to run Christmas parties for those who remained and Village Halls ran cinema entertainments. Villages rang with the sound of Christmas carols interspersed with "Roll out the Barrel" and "There'll always be an England", two additional war songs, roared out in high-pitched children's voices.

Lord Louis Mountbatten had told his father-in-law, a distinguished peer, the story of the recent meeting of the young Prince Philip of Greece, then aged eighteen, and the thirteen-year-old Princess Elizabeth. It seemed that while the King's elder daughter had shown great interest in the brisk and spirited young man in naval uniform, he himself had shown greater interest in the frisky and animated younger sister, then aged nine, who had romped and giggled with him quite unrestrainedly.

On Christmas Day, carrying out the tradition set by his father, the King gave a Christmas broadcast, a message which was to make a historic impact. Choosing words from a collection of poems published by Miss M. L. Haskins, he used the following for the end of his broadcast:

> "I said to the man who stood at the Gate of the Year, 'Give me a light that I may tread safely into the unknown.' And he replied, 'Go out into the darkness, and put your hand into the Hand of God. That shall be to you better than light, and safer than a known way.'"

The extremely courageous Poles were now vanquished.

On New Year's Day 1940, frost had silvered the land, luminous, iridescent, and singularly beautiful. Meanwhile, the Soviet Union had attacked Finland.

Three Baltic states, Latvia, Lithuania and Estonia, fearful of Russia's potential military might, had already bowed down to Soviet control. Finland had refused and had then been overrun by Soviet troops. Aid for Finland became a general cry. A small Anglo-French force was assembled, the French ministers hoping that this might lead to an anti-Bolshevik crusade. Since the signing of the Nazi-Soviet pact, the French had regarded Russia as a prop of Germany. The British Cabinet were said to have dithered. Vague plans were discussed for sending a force to Norway and then on to Sweden with the object of destroying Swedish iron mines and this crippling German industry. The plan was so muddled and confused that no progress was made and on 12th March the Finns suddenly capitulated and made peace with Russia. In France, M. Daladier's collapse as premier was brought about by discontent. He was to be followed by M. Renaud thought to be more resolute. At once Renaud sought an agreement with the British to 'make war and peace in common and not separately'. British public opinion had been much disturbed. Attempting to calm the situation Chamberlain made his famous announcement, "Hitler has missed the bus!"

Hitler's plans, however, were well on target. On 8th April, 1940, the Germans took Denmark unopposed, moving swiftly to Norway seizing every port from Oslo to Narvik and openly defying British sea power. And now, for the British, everything started to go wrong. It was said that the Admiralty and the War office were issuing contradictory orders. Various operations failed disastrously. The aircraft carrier *Glorious* and two destroyers were sunk but the German navy suffered as well. In early May all forces previously landed in great confusion, were withdrawn, bringing the King of Norway and some of his government to England. The country's wrath turned against Chamberlain. Perhaps reaping the reward for his years of solitary warning, Churchill was to find a great public clamour had arisen favouring his replacement with Chamberlain. In the Admiralty the First Lord had said, "We can't guarantee that it will be a better world if we win this war, but it will certainly be a much worse world if we lose."

Strong attacks were now to be made on Chamberlain by the Conservative back-benchers. Ready to resign, Chamberlain put forward the alternative, Lord Halifax. A storm swept through the Commons. Halifax made the modest remark that it would be difficult for a peer to become Prime Minister. Lord Beaverbrook announced, "Churchill is the only saviour." "The decaying men," as Amery had called the Cabinet, "must now face the truth." Lloyd George, now an ageing statesman, echoed the country's desire, "There is only one man, Winston Churchill, who can lead the country to victory in this desperate crisis."

The die was cast. On 10th May Mr Churchill became Prime Minister. A historian wrote later, "In May 1940, Churchill and the British people made a pact with death. They would win the war together, or perish. It was to be victory; victory at all costs, victory in spite of all terror, victory however long and hard the road might be." These words were to chart the history of Britain for the next five years. The country closed ranks behind him.

Now there were to be immense reverses and a whole series of disasters. Before the end of May Germany had conquered the Low Countries, bursting across Belgian territory into France. Churchill flew to Paris three times insisting that the British would fight on, trying to uphold the French morale. His efforts proved in vain, the French premier, Renaud, resigned, and the veteran Marshal Pétain declared that he must sue for an armistice. Holland had collapsed with Queen Wilhelmina, Princess Juliana, Prince Bernhard and two young princesses seeking sanctuary in England.

King Leopold had declined to leave Belgium, now in the grip of Germany. It was soon evident that the situation on the western front was beyond repair. The Germans had attacked through Belgium avoiding the heavy fortifications of the Maginot Line. Lord Gort's expeditionary troops were now almost cut off, their one chance lay in hurried evacuation from the beaches of Dunkirk. An operation known as "Dynamo", a cataclysmic event involving the British navy, together with hundreds of little ships, small craft of every kind manned by volunteers, now began to unfold. With the R.A.F. giving the best possible air cover from bases in England, over three hundred thousand of our troops were saved, together with some French forces, but with overwhelming loss of equipment.

The United Kingdom was now left totally defenceless, but the men had been saved and the country's morale was high. Churchill now warned of hard and heavy tidings, adding the inspiring words, "Never flinch, never weary, never despair."

On 16th June Marshal Pétain sued for an armistice. The terms involved the occupation by German troops of the whole of the Atlantic coast, and the French Government moved its capital to Vichy.

General Charles de Gaulle, who had landed with the troops in England, made clear his determination to organise free French troops to carry on the struggle. French warships at Oran and Dakar were now destroyed by the British navy to prevent them from falling into the enemy's hands.

Britain now had to face immediate threat of invasion. "The crux," said Air Marshal Dowding, "is air superiority." Lord Beaverbrook was appointed Minister of aircraft production, inspiring workers as he had inspired his newspaper production. "Action THIS day" became the new command.

An urgent appeal went out for scrap metal. Gardens lost their railings, and thousands of householders sacrificed aluminium pans. The country was to owe much to Ernest Bevin the new Minister of Labour. Under his forceful personality and confident authority men and women worked for long hours. Wages rose and unemployment disappeared.

An auxiliary force known as Local Defence Volunteers had been hastily inaugurated, soon to be given the more appropriate title of Home Guard. By mid-summer 1940, over a million volunteers had enrolled. For some months their equipment was scanty.

With Mussolini now joining in the war on Hitler's side, Churchill warned the country that a German attack on Britain was imminent. In a speech which was to become historic, the Prime Minister exhorted, "Let us therefore brace ourselves to our duties, and so bear ourselves

General Charles de Gaulle in London, 1940.

that, if the British Empire and its Commonwealth last for a thousand years, men will still say 'This was their finest hour'."

Hitler's immense success had taken him and his High Command by surprise. Still hoping to make peace with the British, he had not made plans for an invasion of the British Isles. While deploring the tragic loss of France, Britain had gained new allies, Poland, Norway, Luxembourg, Holland and Belgium. Soviet Russia and the U.S.A. still remained neutral. Meanwhile Churchill, while still at the Admiralty had begun a correspondence with President Roosevelt. These letters were later to become a vital channel of communication between Britain and the U.S.A. But for the moment, the Americans could do virtually nothing. The British had to face extreme peril on their own. Roosevelt found one loophole, he could certify a number of rifles as "surplus to American requirements". These were supplied much to their delight, to the painfully under-equipped Home Guard. Hitler's invasion plan 'Operation Sea-Lion' could not be long delayed.

Rumours had circulated that the King had not shown much enthusiasm for Churchill's premiership. It was said that he would have preferred Lord Halifax. Very soon, however, as the clouds darkened, the King began to respect his new Prime Minister's vast experience, his unrivalled knowledge of history, his brilliant speeches, his real regard for the monarchy and his unshakable spirit of aggression and optimism. The formal audiences were changed to lunches on Tuesdays and it was not long before a warm friendship formed.

Churchill quoted the words of Dorothy L. Sayers written after the fall of France:

"Praise God, now, for an English war—
The grey tide and the sullen coast,
The menace of the urgent hour,
The single island, like a tower,
Ringed with an angry host.

At the premier's instigation an air raid shelter was constructed at Buckingham Palace, after his suggestion that the Queen and the two princesses should leave, possibly for Canada. "The children can't go without me," the Queen had replied, "I can't leave the King, and the King won't go." The two princesses were, however, installed at Windsor at the King's insistence.

The outlook of both the King and Queen was one of spirited retaliation. After a particularly black week at the time of the Boer War, Queen Victoria is reputed to have ordered, "There will be no talk of defeat and no despondent news discussed in any of MY homes!" Her great-grandson was thought to hold the same views. In fact, firing ranges were set up at Buckingham Palace and it was revealed that monarchy were becoming deadly shots.

On 16th July Hitler directed that, as the British had spurned his hand of friendship, preparations should go forward for the invasion. Our sea defence had been left largely to light cruisers and destroyers. Fighter Command still remained our most vital defence. Immensely fortified anti-tank obstructions had been erected on the eastern and southern beaches.

Even after all these years, little cousin, years before your parents had been born, the memory of that fraught summer still remains searingly vivid. Apprehension was now building up into a climax; then, as the sun's first light turned to gold, illuminating the countryside in a radiant dawn, General Goering's Luftwaffe struck, carrying out the first heavy bombing raids on Southern England. For a month or more German bombing was concentrated on shipping, ports and airfields. By September, what was to become known as 'The Battle of Britain' was approaching its climax. Due to the immense skill and courage and also sacrifice of a few hundred young pilots and their crews, their points of intersection directed by radar, and with superior aircraft, it was shown that greater losses had been inflicted on the Luftwaffe than could be afforded. Having failed to achieve Hitler's plans of overwhelming success in the air, Goering was obliged to withdraw and the fear of invasion faded. This battle in the air proved to be one of the most dramatic actions in the war. Well might Mr Churchill exclaim, "Never in the field of human conflict was so much owed by so many to so few." The FEW were to be triumphantly carried forward to the heights of history.

The war now took on a new shape. The miraculous escape from total disaster at Dunkirk, and the success of the 'Battle of Britain' brought a new surge of confidence in the Prime Minister. His words uttered so emphatically "We will NEVER surrender" dispelled all doubts and fears. Henceforward there seemed to be a unanimous sense of purpose with absolute refusal to contemplate defeat. But there were no delusions. As autumn advanced, with German bombers raining bombs on London and on larger industrial towns civilians found themselves in the front line. A quiet heroism suddenly emerged.

Night bombing was soon to be known in popular parlance as 'the blitz' from the German word-blitzkrieg used by Hitler against Poland. The word "blitz" was an inappropriate choice as there no sign of a lightning war against England. But the word 'took hold'. The British had a hard time to survive throughout the winter of 1940-1941. High explosive and incendiary bombs were now causing great destruction. Soon after Christmas the London docks and dockland appeared to be standing in a sea of flame. So furious were the raids that not only London, but Bristol, Coventry, Sheffield, Hull, Plymouth, Liverpool, Southampton and many others possessed few streets which had not been blackened by fire, roadways a mass of rubble, fallen walls and gutted buildings. Citizens stepped warily over broken glass and notices appeared "When your home has been bombed go to the nearest Air raid shelter. Eat hot potatoes if you can procure them, they are nourishing and warming". While many now slept in underground shelters, brave volunteers remained in the open, fire-watchers, air raid wardens, first aid crews, ambulance drivers, firemen, rescue crews, nurses and police. These courageous and self-sacrificing citizens took no heed of their own safety in these perilous times. Factories had been dispersed, but fortunately the effect on production proved to be less than had been feared. King George the Sixth and Queen Elizabeth were quickly on the scene after a serious raid, often accompanied by the Prime Minister. Even Buckingham Palace had now been bombed allowing the Queen to say, "I'm glad we've been bombed, now I can look the East End in the face." An unknown American admirer had sent the Queen a little verse which had touched her deeply. It ran:

> Be it said to your renown
> That you wore your gayest gown,
> Your bravest smile, and stayed in Town
> When London Bridge was burning down.

Led by their King and Queen, the unshaken spirit of the British remained unbroken, but there were many setbacks still to come.

The scene of engagement for the British forces had now shifted to the Mediterranean. The Italian Marshal Graziani had invaded Egypt from Libya. General Wavell counter attacked pushing the Italians west of

Benghazi and taking many prisoners. Italian armaments, despite Mussolini's bluster, were said to be poor and it was reported that Italian will to fight was shaky. From Kenya and the Sudan British columns were advancing against Mussolini's cruelly acquired East African Empire. Soon the British were to take Eritrea, the Italian Somaliland and Abyssinia, at last avenging Mussolini's defiance of the League of Nations in the 1930s. Later, the British navy inflicted heavy losses on the Italian fleet. With Italy suffering reverses it was obvious that the Germans would intervene, causing many British casualties. With their immense air strength German forces now overcome British troops in Greece as well as in Crete, soon turning their attention to an attack on Malta.

The relentless months rolled on. Clothes rationing had been introduced and food rationing became tighter. Acres of grass had been given over to the 'Dig for Victory' campaign.

The United States Lend-Lease Act now authorized President Roosevelt to put American surplus resources at British disposal on the grounds that this was now regarded as security for America's future. This gave Britain most urgently needed supplies regardless of her ability to pay in dollars. "Give us the tools," Mr Churchill had requested, "and we will finish the job." Many Americans were determined to remain neutral, still doubting British ability to win the war. The R.A.F. were now carrying out devastating reciprocal air raids into the heart of Germany. A brave resistance movement was now gathering strength in occupied France, also in Holland, but the news remained cripplingly severe.

On the night of 10th May, 1941, a year after he had become Prime Minister, Churchill stood in the ruins of the House of Commons, tears in his eyes, grinding his walking stick into the dust and rubble. The Commons moved to the House of Lords, and the peers were given space in Church House, Westminster. With the Axis Powers now occupying the whole of the Baltic Peninsula, a treaty was made with Turkey guaranteeing Turkish neutrality. German air strenght was now directed against both Malta and Gibraltar. Submarine and mining attacks continued on trans-Atlantic shipping. British naval strength was painfully stretched while millions of tons of supplies to Britain were lost. This was the bitter time which Churchill referred to as "The Battle of the Atlantic".

Meanwhile a green and golden spring had given way to a perfect

St Paul's after the "Blitz", 1941.

summer. The maverick bird, the cuckoo, was calling lustily, cherry trees had flowered and waned, canopies of floral loveliness. In the ruins of pitiful bomb damage flowers and weeds began to bloom, seeds dropped by the wind. Nature took no heed of man's stupidity. On midsummer eve, in an almost opaque twilight with skylarks still hovering, the spectacular news was given to the country that Hitler had launched an attack on the Soviet Union. At once the Prime Minister's voice was heard over a crackling radio, "We must give unreserved, solidarity with the people of Soviet Russia," he declared. Now events gained monetum like a herd of stampeding elephants. Labour was to be directed and allocated, some young men being sent into the mines. All women from 18-40 were obliged to register. General Wavell launched an offensive in Egypt against the German General Rommel which proved a failure, British tanks had proved less than adequate. General Wavell was moved to India and his place in the Middle East was taken by General Sir Claude Auchinleck.

General Auchinleck, now looking with great apprehension at the line of the Caucasus postponed his desert offensive, believing, as did many, that Russia would be overcome. Churchill may have shared the same fears for he spoke again, "The Russian danger is our danger, and the danger of the United States, just as the cause of any Russian fighting for his heart and home is the cause of free people in every quarter of the globe." In his book *The Second World War* Churchill had added, "If Hitler invaded Hell I would make at least a favourable reference to the Devil in the House of Commons!"

Fear of Communism now had to be laid aside for the duration.

In August the Prime Minister and President Roosevelt held a meeting off the coast of Newfoundland. The new Atlantic Alliance created the machinery for further mercantile and marine help, greatly assisting the British and the exiled Governments of Western Europe. The prospect was totally transformed again when, on 7th December, 1941, the Japanese bombed the United States naval base at Pearl Harbour. All the doubts of the American people were resolved for them when they found themselves in the war, no longer European but world wide.

Taking advantage of the European war, creeping up like a menacing shadow, the Japanese had pressed into French Indo-China, Malaya and the Dutch East Indies. When they reached the fringe of Singapore Churchill had sent the battleship *Prince of Wales* and the battle cruiser *Repulse* but with too few aircraft. Both were sunk. Hitler pledged his support to Japan declaring war on the U.S.A. This enabled Roosevelt to establish the principal that Germany must be defeated before Japan, relieving the Prime Minister of his worst nightmare, an all-out war in the Far East.

As 1942 opened, it became evident that the tale of reverses was not yet over. Singapore fell. The Japanese invaded and overcome Burma. They also established themselves on many strategic Pacific Islands. In North Africa General Rommel had captured Tobruk and was advancing towards El Alamein making preparations to capture Egypt. The Russians, fighting desperately, still held the key cities of Leningrad, Moscow, Sebastopol, and Stalingrad. One of the worst winters thought to be in living memory was now to descend on the German invaders.

Great Britain and the United States now merged together in a conference named 'Arcadia' to cement Anglo-American partnership. It was generally believed that all the Code names introduced into the war

President Franklin D. Roosevelt.

Field-Marshal Viscount Montgomery of Alamein.

campaign were suggested by the Prime Minister as a result of his unique imagination and exceptional literary gifts. A joint committee was suggested which Roosevelt widened into Combined Chiefs of Staff. Life was becoming much harsher. Coal was strictly controlled and food became sparse. But there was one asset, the radio. "Music while you work" and many nonsense programmes relayed to factories could be heard not only by civilians and the Home Guard, but by the wounded in hospital, a large part of the navy and Air Force, and by many servicemen overseas. For those who demanded something more sophisticated a Brains' Trust was formed and listeners sent in questions. There was further cultural activity, lunch time concerts, and an elaborate enterprise called CEMA (Council for the encouragement of music and the arts). People from completely different social backgrounds seemed to feel themselves welded into one community. Threadbare sheets and blankets became shabbier.

Shortages were country wide, even for royalty. Small luxuries like aluminium kettles and rubber hot water bottles had vanished. Even metal hair pins were unprocurable, known as kirbigrips. When Mrs Eleanor Roosevelt visited the King and Queen in the autumn of 1942, staying at Buckingham Palace, she gave this description afterwards to her daughter: "The Queen herself drew my black-out curtains, apologising for the very small fire in my grate. These royal folk share all the hardships of the British people. They may only draw hot water into the bath at a five inch level. They mend all their own clothes, even their linen sheets had been patched but they gave me the best blankets. The palace is an immense place, terribly draughty. With so little heating, I don't known how they will keep the damp out of the walls. A bomb fell on them and this damage has been patched up temporarily. The Queen was so thankful that no one had been hurt. The blown out windows have been covered with wooden boards. The whole place is depressing and dimly lit. Their food is sparse, nothing that the ordinary public cannot have. We have seen Mr and Mrs Churchill. He was wearing what the public call 'a siren suit'. He himself exclaimed, 'Clemmie (Mrs Churchill) bought me these rompers, they are very comfortable.' He smiled like a cherub when he heard that General Montgomery had begun to advance towards El Alamein. The two young daughters are quite different, the elder very serious, old for her years, devoted to her father and shares his outdoor interest in sport. The younger vivacious and bouncy but inclined to pout. When she heard that she was to wear a cut down coat of her sister's refashioned in her size she was much upset. 'Talk it over with Mummy,' her father advised. They are just like any ordinary family."

As autumn darkened, General Sir Bernard Montgomery (Field Marshal Viscount), a man of resolution and decisiveness with intense clarity of purpose, led the British Eighth Army to victory, routing General Rommel's Afrika Corps.

And now, under the command of the American General Dwight D. Eisenhower, a joint British and American army invaded French North Africa. At long last, it seemed that the tide was beginning to turn. Allied land forces, however, still faced strong counter attacks from Tunisia where strong German troops had gathered. The battle of Tunisia proved to be a triumph of joint operation, General Montgomery's forces from Libya and combined Anglo-American and French forces under General Alexander.

The completion of this brilliant campaign exposed what Churchill had always referred to as "the soft under-belly of the Axis" enabling the American Seventh and the British Eighth armies to land on the coast of Sicily at length pressing forward to Italy.

In Russia, what had become known as the Battle of Stalingrad, beating back the German forces, had made an immense contribution towards the eventual defeat of Germany.

In January 1943, Churchill and Roosevelt, with their staff and advisers met at Casablanca. General de Gaulle did not accompany them, although he was now regarded as the sole leader of resurgent France. American strength was growing massively. Churchill recognised that British strength was burning low.

The year sped on, with nature again providing the exquisite beauty of unfolding trees, the colourful loveliness of summer gardens, and the dappled woodland pastures.

On 25th July Mussolini was deposed by the Fascist Grand Council. The King of Italy commissioned Marshal Badoglio to form a new Government.

Meanwhile, Churchill had managed to visit both Cairo and Moscow grabbing the chance of acting as intermediary between the East and the West. Roosevelt had produced the terms for ending the war, 'Unconditional surrender'. Churchill endorsed the phrase.

It was to be a long, hard struggle for the British and American forces to fight their way to Rome against Italians strongly reinforced by fresh

Mr Winston Churchill outside 10 Downing Street, 1943, in buoyant mood.

German troops. This campaign proved to be much tougher than had been supposed.

The Americans were now demanding that everything should be subordinated to preparations for a second front. Many troops in Britain were now to be pinned down to take part in 'Overlord' the campaign shortly to be undertaken as a massive invasion of Northern France.

Mr Churchill, the British Prime Minister, was now a very tired man. Pneumonia had taken its toll. The British people had risen to extreme heights of courage, sacrifice and resolution, they too were tiring. The last months of 1943 and first months of 1944 were to be the final test. British bombers, now accompanied by the U.S. Air Force were carrying out massive attacks on German industrial towns. At the end of 1943, Roosevelt and Churchill met Stalin at Teheran. General Eisenhower had been appointed supreme commander of the second front.

1944 opened with British and American forces still deadlocked in Italy. Meanwhile immense preparations were going forward for operation 'Overlord'. Artificial harbours known as 'Mulberries' were being designed, together with a special pipeline called 'Pluto' (Pipe Line Under the Ocean) built to carry oil under the English Channel. When the Allied landing took place in Northern France on 6th June, 1944 it inaugurated one of the great milestones in British history.

A few weeks before, the Germans launched their secret weapon, pilotless aircraft, exploding on landing and causing widespread damage. Many of these were launched from the coast of France, contemptuously dismissed as "Doodlebugs" a word invented by newspapers. The public took them seriously, together with the rockets which followed. Londoners who had endured so much were openly fearful. As the Allies advanced in France the rocket launching sites were destroyed.

Now it had become a question of time. With overwhelming American help, the U-Boats had been mastered. The Americans had also put into the air a long-range fighter greatly superior to any fighter produced by Germany. In addition, Russia, in spite of suffering catastrophic losses, was on the point of a fierce counter attack against Germany.

Camouflaged tank in France, 1944.

For the D-Day operation immense forces had been gathered. General Eisenhower, the supreme commander, selected General Montgomery, brought back from Italy, to command the initial landings. He had also chosen British Air and Naval commanders, Tedder and Ramsay. Most elaborate plans had been developed to deceive the Germans. A non-existent army had been built up in the south-east of England and dummy craft assembled. Wireless messages were poured out. Hitler was said to have felt uncertain. "You should never under-estimate the British," he said, "they have enormous staying power and ingenuity".

By July, after many setbacks and a tragically large number of casualties, Canadians, British and Americans broke through the German armour and began the vast sweep through France. With many German forces encircled, the Allies stormed forward over the river Seine. On 25th August Paris was liberated. General de Gaulle established his authority amid scenes of frantic rejoicing. Parachutists were then sent forward to seize bridges over the Rhine. Churchill and the hard-pressed British sensed that the end of the war was in sight. As Churchill expressed it, "But for the 'Few' how nearly we could have lost." Instructions were given to let the public enjoy the beaches, for the first time for five years. Volunteers came forward eagerly to help move the immense fortifications hurriedly erected against invasion.

By the end of 1944, France Belgium and Holland had been liberated. Italy had also fallen to the Allies, this brilliant achievement eclipsed by the stupendous Second Front.

In July 1944 an event took place which was to prove that by no means every German supported Hitler. It transpired that Germans of different political persuasions and social backgrounds joined with military leaders in planning an assassination attempt on Hitler's life by placing a bomb-filled briefcase at the foot of Hitler's place in the map room of the East Prussian Headquarters. Had it succeeded it would have killed the German Führer, sweeping the Nazis from power and shortening the war by many months. A colonel's search for more leg room under the map table had pushed Colonel Claus von Stauffenberg's briefcase, already prepared, farther from the Führer's position with the result that, while this colonel, two generals, and a shorthand-writer were killed, Hitler himself escaped with minor burns, a lacerated hand and badly damaged clothing. The leader of this plot, Colonel Count Claus Schenk von Stauffenberg, to give him his full name, set off for Berlin, confident that their attempt had succeeded. Their hope was short-lived.

He and his fellow conspirators, chased to Berlin by troops loyal to Hitler, were shot immediately by firing squad, said to be carried out in the glare of a car's headlamps.

The Führer's revenge was merciless and savage. Hundreds of arrests were made, both soldiers and civilians. A mock trial was staged followed by cruel torture lasting many weeks before death by strangulation. The victims were stripped of clothes and left dangling on loops of piano wire attached to butchers' hooks, some taking half an hour to die. These executions were filmed in detail for Hitler to gloat over in his Berchtesgaden retreat.

The Gestapo, Secret Police (from the German word Geheime Staatspolizei) were ordered to arrest anyone remotely connected with the plot, even those who had taken no part but had heard about it. Once arrested there was no escape from torture and gruesome execution.

Even Stalin was said to have been shocked by this inhuman barbarity.

Through the autumn of 1944, the Allied forces in the west were holding a very thin line. Confident of success Hitler gave orders for a powerful offensive but the Americans were very strong in resistance. General Eisenhower gave General Montgomery temporary command. By Christmas the German advance had been checked. There was now considerable disagreement between British and American Chiefs of Staff some fearing that victory in the west seemed to be receding.

Early in February 1945, Churchill, Roosevelt and Stalin met at Yalta on the Black Sea coast of the Crimea. Roosevelt succeeded in gaining Stalin's agreement to enter the war against Japan while Churchill secured Russian approval for the eventual creation of French, British, Soviet and American zones in occupied Germany. Stalin agreed that the 'Curzon Line' settled as a Russo-Polish frontier by Lloyd George and the Foreign Secretary, Lord Curzon, in 1920, should be accepted again as a definite frontier between the future Polish and Soviet Governments.

Those present at this conference had noticed an increasing frailty in President Roosevelt's physical strength.

The chiefs of British Air staff, Portal, Tedder and Harris, had concluded that one further devastating onslaught against German strategic targets, including towns, might cause morale, already crumbling under the Russian offensive, to collapse. If the air attack aided the Russians it would help to shorten the war. Early in March,

American forces crossed the Rhine. Two weeks later Montgomery's forces had penetrated into the Ruhr. General Alexander's forces had now reached the valley of the Po river.

As the eighth army were sweeping into Austria, President Roosevelt died. Harry S. Truman became the new President of the United States.

On 28th April, Mussolini and his mistress were shot by Communists, their bodies hung upside down secured to the side of a garage. Hitler in his Berlin bunker, horrified at the hideous end of his fellow European dictator, married Eva Braun, his woman companion of many years, then gave instructions that both their bodies were to be cremated. The remains, found by the Russians, were subsequently destroyed. At last, the wicked tyrant was no more.

On 4th May, German forces in north-western Germany surrendered unconditionally to General Montgomery. Three days later Admiral Doenitz, Hitler's successor, signed the surrender instrument on all fronts at General Eisenhower's headquarters. German forces in Italy had also surrendered unconditionally to General Alexander. On 8th May, the Western Allies celebrated V-E Day (Victory in Europe) with delirious rejoicing. The two houses of Parliament proceeded to St Margaret's, Westminster, to give thanks for victory, while church bells rang, floodlights replaced the black-out and wildly shouting and singing crowds danced in the streets.

Outside Buckingham Palace the crowd was shouting, "We want the King, we want the Queen." At length the Royal couple emerged, the King a slight frail figure. Beside him stood his daughters, Princess Elizabeth in A.T.S. uniform. Very soon Mr Churchill joined them. A crescendo of cheers greeted him. For many minutes the cheers resounded from Constitution Hill all along the Mall. Aircraft were dropping flares and coloured lights. Balloons appeared, saved from before the war for this unique occasion. The cheers grew tumultuous. A newspaper leader, printed the following morning, described the scene, "King George the Sixth, Queen Elizabeth and the Prime Minister, Mr Winston Churchill, were accorded the greatest victory reception since Napoleon returned from Austerlitz".

In the meantime, the war in the Far East still had to be won.

For the moment, however, to the wildly cavorting revellers in Trafalgar Square, lustily singing 'The White Cliffs of Dover' victory in Europe seemed enough to be going on with.

Dead silence fell when the King and Queen attended a National Service of Thanksgiving at St Paul's Cathedral with the public standing at attention listening to the unbearably poignant notes of the Last Post sounded by a solitary trumpeter evoking the memory of the many millions who had lost their lives in this grievous and heartrending war.

To his mother, the veteran Queen Mary, the King wrote: "We have been overwhelmed by all the kind things people have said and written to us thanking us for our part in the war effort. Elizabeth and I only tried to do our duty as you and Papa did. How grateful I feel that this cruel war is over, at least in Europe."

For you, my very young relation, born in the 1980s, the Hitler war will emerge like a mummified spidery banner left over from long ago, but the roots of the present rest in the past; step by step every generation takes its share. The wounds heal, birds sing where once shells exploded, cattle graze and new trees grow. Battered cities are torn down and replaced by new. Another world dawns and the tolling of the funeral bell means little to those who were not born.

As Mr Churchill expressed it 'Nostalgia is not a programme'. The busy summer of 1945 now rode on.

Looking into the future, the Prime Minister added, "We must never let the nation overpay itself beyond its true income."

The apple orchards were now alive with blossom, and in the towns, the newly lit street lamps, after so many years of black-out darkness, seemed to glow like golden flowers.

The tide of Allied defeat in the Pacific had begun to turn. Australian and American troops had advanced well into New Guinea while Rangoon had been retaken. In Burma, the torrid heat of jungle warfare and the intolerable climate had placed a hideous strain on all participants and it was being rumoured that the Japanese were treating their prisoners with exceptional cruelty. In the meantime, a new South-East Asia Command to be led by Admiral Lord Louis Mountbatten had been set up.

Scientists in America were believed to have informed President Truman, that, should the need arise, atomic bombs would be ready for use by the late summer.

On 18th May, the Prime Minister had proposed to the Labour and Liberal parties that the coalition Government should continue until the end of the Japanese war. He had been warmly backed by Bevin, but Clement Attlee, the Labour leader, offered to continue only for a further six months. Churchill could not agree and resigned, bringing the National Government to an end. A General Election was called for early July.

The electors, only too thankful now to get back to their own lives were not stirred to display any feelings of revenge against Germany. In fact there was no interest at all in Foreign affairs, they wanted housing, jobs, good educational facilities and the new programme of which they had heard so much, the welfare state and social security.

As Churchill toured the country in an open car, making his famous two-fingered 'V' (Victory) sign, he was tumultuously cheered, but the electorate voted against him. The election result produced a striking victory for Labour.

The King now sent for Clement Attlee who moved into 10 Downing Street as the new Labour Prime Minister. In earlier days no one could have foreseen this quiet undemonstrative man, who spoke in clipped sentences, as Prime Ministerial quality. It was said jokingly that Attlee always used no words when one would do! At the end of his life this little rhyme was published:

"Few thought he was even a starter,
There were many who thought themselves smarter,
Yet, he ended P.M., C.H., and O.M.
An Earl, and a Knight of the Garter."

It was a warm tribute for a man who was now to bear the brunt of many formidable years.

The circumstances of Japanese surrender now had ominous consequences for the future of the entire world.

On 6th August an atomic bomb was dropped on the city of Hiroshima destroying more than half the city area and causing something like 80,000 deaths and an even greater number of casualties. Two days later, faithful to his promise, Stalin declared war on Japan by invading Manchuria. On 9th August, the Americans dropped a second atomic bomb of a different type on the naval base of Nagasaki. Five days later the Japanese Cabinet, pressed by Emperor Hirohito, accepted 'unconditional surrender'. Everywhere in the Pacific, Japanese forces surrendered.

On 15th August, 'V-J' Day (Victory against Japan) was at last achieved but the world had been so shocked by the appalling description of the two bombed Japanese cities that rejoicing took place in a minor key.

Distressed privately, but taking his electoral defeat with outward equinimity, Mr Churchill made his last war-time statement—"Now at last," he said, "we are able to pause in thankfulness and take hope that, with victory on all three fronts, and in all three elements, there might finally develop a safe and happy future for tormented mankind." He then left for a holiday, with painting equipment among his luggage.

Perhaps I may break off for a moment to introduce a brief personal note quoting a letter written to my father. This excerpt symbolizes the desperately shabby England of the last months of 1945. As a Major in the Women's Service then known as A.T.S. (Auxiliary Territorial Service) I had undertaken to remain in uniform for an additional six months to help with the intricacies of what had been named 'The Army Educational Release Scheme'. Accordingly, I had been instructed to report to Liverpool, after a brief leave in Hampshire with my father, now a widower. The year was closing in and November daylight soon drained out of the sky. I wrote: "The train (from Euston to Liverpool) took seven hours. There was no food but a kindly member of the W.V.S. provided me with a spam sandwich at Crewe. I would have loved tea but the queues were so long the train jolted forward before I could get anywhere near the crowded buffet. With the black-out lifted we were hoping for a well-lit city, but Liverpool was in complete darkness, electricity had failed. An obliging R.E.M.E. Captain helped me heave my case to the station exit. There were no taxis. A fellow passenger informed me that buses only ran once an hour. A bustling News van passed and the driver offered me a lift to the hotel. I was very grateful. Dinner was finished but an elderly sympathetic waiter told me he could fix me up with a dried egg omelet. He brought me two tinned apricots and a small portion of cheese. There was no butter, and sugar and milk had run out. I endured black coffee but the meal had tasted like a banquet—I felt so hungry! The bedroom towel was the size of a face flannel, and soap tablet as slim as a razor blade. Sheets were very torn, lying in strips, and blankets threadbare."—It is difficult to remember, looking back, that I was staying in Liverpool's leading hotel. War years had taken their toll. Even so, by the end of 1945, despite shortages, the whole population seemed to be awaiting a rising peacetime sun. .

The days whirled along, soon crowding into weeks, months, and before long, years. Mr Attlee's Government was to achieve much that was essential in recovery and reconstruction, laying the foundation for the growth of the National Health Service and the newly thought out Welfare State. By degrees, the demobilization of many thousands of service men and service women was carried out smoothly, while industry became gradually converted to peace time production. A new word, automation, the introduction of new technology, began to be heard.

The abrupt ending of Lend-Lease immediately after the defeat of Japan, forced the new Labour Chancellor to bring in harsh measures to avoid a grave financial crisis. The Americans had generously agreed to financial help, known as Marshall Aid, from General Marshall's plan to assist Europe's recovery from the dislocation of war, a project gratefully received. The Soviet Government rejected this help but the Western Powers set up a body shortly to become known as O.E.E.C. Organisation for European Economic Co-operation. Shortages were to continue for many years and those who paraded 'black-market' spoils had become known as 'Spivs', widely despised.

Throughout 1946 there was a huge government drive to produce new houses. The rehabilitation of bombed out cities was urgent. Several

Pre-fabs at Gretna Green. The post-war effort to meet the country-wide housing shortage.

thousand temporary pre-fabricated houses had sprung up, while, to save valuable space, the municipal councils began to plan high rise flats. With the bull-dozing of old familiar communities, those housed in high rise flats found themselves faced with a frightening loss of identity and a sense of horrifying loneliness. Mothers too high to keep an eye on children found hostile neighbours; soon the lifts became vandalized, elderly occupants could no longer climb the stairs. It was a time of intensive legislative activity intimately affecting the daily lives of the ordinary citizen, sometimes for good, but frequently for ill.

The great year of crisis, 1947, opened with an exceptionally severe winter. A fuel crisis forced many cuts in electricity, seriously interrupted production and transport, and hampered the signal drive for exports so urgently needed. The public, still accustomed to war measures, accepted the austerity, the strictly rationed petrol and food. Clothing, too, remained scarce. Coupons from the ration books had to be handed over for every new garment. As in the war years, 'Make do and Mend' flourished. The cold remained intense. The Labour party could however, congratulate themselves, that inflation was still under control, and that, by and large full employment was still being maintained.

During the worst of the bombing raids a phrase had been coined "Britain can take it". Now wits were changing this into "Britain can't have it!" The arctic winter lasted until the end of March.

In Nuremberg, the trials of the major Nazi war criminals, presided over by American, British, French and Soviet judges, were reaching their end. Twenty-five had been sentenced to death and many more to imprisonment. Goering alone escaped the hangman by swallowing a phial of poison a few hours before execution. A very obese man, it was thought that he had hidden the phial in a fold of flesh. Rudolf Hess, now the sole prisoner in the four-power-controlled Spandau prison, Hitler's Deputy, had flown from Augsburg to Scotland in the spring of 1941, apparently on his own initiative, in the hope of securing a negotiated peace. He had stipulated on arrival that the peace negotiations should not include Churchill. The British interned him until the Nuremberg trials.

The Government now went ahead with an intensive programme of nationalisation, the Bank of England, Mines, Railways, Canals, Road Haulage, Iron and Steel, with national Boards appointed to manage each concern. Defects of this programme soon became apparent.

The Cinema was still gaining in strength, retaining great popularity. It had become noticeable that the film industry had gradually introduced a number of new names into school registers. Among boys, Christian names like Dirk, Clint, Clark, Spencer, Gregory, Kirk, Cary and Burt, were not uncommon, while girls had blossomed into Myrna, Greta, Greer, Hedy, Lana, Marilyn, Claudette and Ava, formerly quite unusual.

The public responded very happily to the announcement of an engagement between Princess Elizabeth and Prince Philip of Greece, whose autumn wedding was received with immense enthusiasm.

Queen Mary and the Royal family were still eating what the Americans referred to as 'Utility meals'. On V-E Day, the King had detailed a group of young officers to escort his daughters out of the Palace to mingle with the crowd. The throngs of merry-makers revelling in the brightly lit streets did not recognise them. It was said that they were even taken to travel on an underground train thought to be a rapturous experience. "Poor darlings," wrote the King, "they have never had any fun yet."

Prince Philip's real name was very cumbersome, Schleswig-Holstein-Sonderburg-Glucksburg. As his mother had been a Mountbatten, wisely he had chosen to call himself Lieutenant Mountbatten.

Winston Churchill, now back in Parliament as leader of the Opposition, refreshed after a long holiday, made a characteristic comment, "In this year of bitter winter, continued rationing, and the tragedy of the loss of India which we are soon to see, this engagement bursts like a light from another world, a flash of pure colour."

The public celebrated with their young "fairy princess" and her handsome groom—presents were now to arrive from all over the world. Queen Mary said, "She is more than just my granddaughter, she is our future." Like other grandmothers, all her clothing coupons were given to the bride. Mr Churchill added, "Birth and history have thrust great burdens upon her."

In those days before television, the public flocked to the small News Cinemas, erected now in many parts of London and in some of the outer areas, to watch scenes of the Royal wedding. These compact news theatres ran reels of news collected from many parts of the world, also displaying cheerful cartoons and a number of quite instructive programmes.

A few months later, it was the news reels which instructed the public

The Royal family at the wedding of H.R.H. Princess Elizabeth and Lieutenant Philip Mountbatten, R.N.

that independence had been granted to India. There were many images of the last Viceroy, Lord Louis Mountbatten, who was about to become the first Governor General. His wife, the former Hon. Edwina Ashley, was respected for her indefatigable work carried out for the Red Cross.

Sir Stafford Cripps, the Labour Chancellor of the Exchequer, said to be a man of prim and puritanical personality, won political eminence with his austerity programmes. The British balance of trade figures improved. Meanwhile, the British Foreign Secretary, Mr Ernest Bevin, pointed out that, while not overlooking the emergence of the new Commonwealth, Britain now needed to focus her main attention on Europe. An organisation termed U.N.R.R.A. United Nations Relief and Rehabilitation Administration, had been formed to supply help and relieve starvation in Italy, Greece, Poland and Yugoslavia greatly assisting these states to reconstruct their industrial and agricultural economy. All these states were surrounded by potential communists. The prestige of Josip Broz Tito, Marshal of Yugoslavia, had enabled him to defy Stalin refusing to follow a policy dictated by Moscow. Later he was elected President. The Red Army had taken over Rumania and Bulgaria. The United States had sent a naval task-force into the Mediterranean enabling Turkey to resist Soviet Diplomatic pressure. Bevin had greeted the plan for Marshall Aid as 'a lifeline to a sinking man', but Stalin made clear that he had no interest in the recovery of Europe. An impulse had now given rise to a "United States of Europe".

Mr Churchill's famous speech delivered at Fulton, Missouri, in which he warned that 'an iron curtain was descending across Europe' brought a new term into diplomacy.

In May 1948 a 'Congress of Europe' took place in Holland with Churchill as the principal speaker. Many European delegations attended, including, significantly, West Germany. The congress determined to create a European Assembly. Labour leaders were not keen on European integration and in Britain the idea was shouldered aside. After the Soviet coup in Czechoslovakia followed by the currency reform in East Berlin, which led to the famous Berlin Airlift, American leaders stressed that more would need to be done to bring about the future security of Europe. This laid the foundation for the establishment of the North Atlantic Treaty Organisation, N.A.T.O., to be signed a year later by the Foreign Ministers of Belgium, Great Britain, Canada, Denmark, France, Iceland, Italy, Netherlands, Norway, Portugal, and the United States of America. This treaty was to provide for mutual assistance should any one member of the Alliance be attacked. At a later date, Greece, Turkey, and the German Federal Republic were to become N.A.T.O. signatories. There were now two diametrically opposed systems in Europe and the U.S.A., communism and capitalism, this clash had become known as 'The cold war'.

President Truman declared, "If a treaty like N.A.T.O. had existed in 1914 and 1939 supported by all the nations represented today, I believe it would have prevented the aggression leading to both world wars."

In the early morning of Sunday, 14th November, 1948, crowds were drawn to Buckingham Palace. Before the official posting of a bulletin on the Palace railings, news had already reached the waiting throng that Princess Elizabeth had presented her husband, the Duke of Edinburgh, with a son. A mass of roses and carnations from hothouses were seen disappearing through the Palace gates, loudly cheered by onlookers.

The now disbanded E.N.S.A., Entertainments National Service Association, a body which had provided entertainments of all sorts, for troops at home and abroad, had also given the B.B.C. a number of very popular broadcasters. Names like Harry Secombe, Jimmy Edwards, Richard Murdoch, Kenneth Horne, Hattie Jacques, Eric Sykes, and a host more were turning into a kind of national background.

In the theatre, experienced leading actors and actresses were re-appearing, Emlyn Williams, Cecil Parker, Eric Portman, Michael Redgrave, Wendy Hiller, Gwen Ffrangcon Davies, Fay Compton, Margaret Rawlings, Madeleine Carroll, Athene Seyler, Alec Guinness, Edmund Gwenn, Celia Johnson, Malcolm Keen, Basil Sydney, to name but a very small number of those who had given much pleasure to 1930s theatre audiences. Many new young stars were bustling forward.

The last year of the tempestuous 1940s was now dawning. It was soon seen that the threat of Communist expansion which so menaced the countries of Europe was being strongly felt in Asia. The victory of the Chinese Communists in their civil war against General Chiang Kai-shek had transformed the political situation in neighbouring countries. The Communist forces of North Korea invaded the South. The United Nations intervened in order to save the South Koreans. The British supported America by sending a small contingent of troops who became involved in a thoroughly unpleasant and, in the end, inconclusive war. British forces had been withdrawn from Palestine after the population had become uncontrollable. The bitter war between Jews and Arabs finally ended in an independent Jewish State, Israel. The Arabs were never to come to terms with this outcome.

As a result of all these overseas difficulties, the Government agreed to prolong National Service for young men reaching eighteen, for a period of two years for each serviceman.

Very soon N.A.T.O. comprising all the powers of the European Atlantic Seaboard, with the exception of Eire and Spain set up a supreme Headquarters of Allied Powers, known as S.H.A.P.E. with General Eisenhower, much respected by Europeans, appointed the first Supreme Commander.

Meanwhile in the Far East, General Chiang Kai-Shek became a President in Formosa (Taiwan) as Peking fell to the Communists. He had hoped for American intervention but President Truman was not prepared to become involved. He was never again to gain a footing on the Chinese mainland but rejoiced to watch Taiwan enjoy prosperity through her close economic link with the United States.

By the end of 1949, the Labour Administration had granted independence to India, Pakistan, Ceylon and Burma. The Welfare State had been accepted, and while the Conservatives were now being looked upon as people of moderation, some Socialists had become class warriors. Aneurin Bevan declaimed that the "Tories were lower than vermin"; Mrs Bessie Braddock proclaimed, "I don't care if the non-working-class starve to death." This gave Lord Beaverbrook the chance of commenting, "Is Labour really constructing a new and much more humane society?"

A General Election took place in February 1950, with Labour's overall majority being reduced to five. Churchill had persisted in his view that "we should have another talk with Soviet Russia upon the highest level in a supreme effort to end the hatred and manoeuvres of the Cold War." Churchill was now in his 77th year. The Labour party leaders were also ageing. Herbert Morrison had taken the place of Ernest Bevin as Foreign Secretary. Britain was now to face mounting difficulties in both Iran and Egypt.

A happy home event took place in the summer of 1950 when Princess Elizabeth's daughter, Anne, arrived as a sister to the young Prince Charles. Queen Mary was said to have arrived at Buckingham Palace in great delight.

Queen Mary's love of visiting the theatre was well known. Shortly after the birth of Princess Anne, the veteran Queen Mother, (as she was then) expressed a wish to see the unique one-woman show of Ruth Draper, who was appearing for a short public recital at a small theatre, appropriately called 'The Royalty'. Queet Mary, had, of course, admired Ruth Draper's remarkable performances on many earlier occasions. The Lady-in-Waiting who accompanied the Queen wrote a letter to a friend from which I quote:

"We spent an absolutely rapturous afternoon. Before the matinée we listened to the delightful 'tea-time' music played by a competent orchestra almost invisible under a sea of palms. When the curtain rose the stage was almost empty, just a sofa, two chairs and a small table. Ruth Draper then transformed the stage into her own amazing world of imagination. She took us everywhere, a childrens' party, a wedding, a bedroom scene, on board a liner, a holiday in Rome, a garden, the Zoo, a school party visiting the National Gallery, a New York First Night, and a hospital scene. Her imaginary people were so real it was difficult to believe that that one grave, simple woman was alone on the stage.

She was brought round to see us after the performance, telling us that she had 'talked to herself' as a small child. Her famous monologues must be unsurpassed."

The rearmament programme for the Korean war led to a rise in expenditure. The cost of raw materials and the shipping prices were increasing. Mr Hugh Gaitskell had now replaced Sir Stafford Cripps as Chancellor of the Exchequer. Declaring that it was essential to make economies, Mr Gaitskell placed a fifty per cent charge on the formerly free dentures and spectacles provided by the National Health Service. This led to a Labour party crisis. The flamboyant Aneurin Bevan resigned, followed by an important member of the Labour Cabinet, Mr Harold Wilson. The Prime Minister asked for a dissolution of Parliament.

In the General Election which followed in September 1951, the trend moved to the Conservatives with Mr Churchill, now almost seventy-seven, returning again to 10 Downing Street after a gap of six years. Now a number of much younger House of Commons men were to find themselves placed in key administrative posts. Mr R. A. Butler had become Chancellor of the Exchequer and the energetic Mr Harold Macmillan had taken over the Housing Ministry.

In private the British had now almost reached the stage of being able to produce their own atomic bomb.

In America, President Truman, who had gained a surprising victory in the 1948 Presidential Election, had switched the U.S.A. to positive anti-Communism.

This was mid-century, the epoch of your own parents who will probably be able to relate their own memories of the 1950s, 60s and 70s. For those approaching middle age, the creation of the Festival of Britain on a South Thames site was perhaps an outstanding mid-century turning point. This was said to have been the dividing line between the war and the post-war years. The Festival was designed and built to show visitors what Britain was capable of producing as soon as the abominable shortage of materials had been overcome. Architects were given their first major opportunity since the war to show what they could create. A spectacular Concert Hall was erected, together with a National Film Theatre. At a much later date, a National Theatre was planned to serve a new generation.

As economic controls and restrictions became loosened, post-war films and London theatre productions boomed. The competition of television was very near. The early 'espresso' coffee shops were popular. Exciting American musicals such as 'Oklahoma' and 'Annie get your Gun' had crossed the Atlantic and were prospering. A BBC Third programme had been introduced. The Edinburgh Festival of Music and Drama had now become an annual feature.

In Buckingham Palace, a sad event was developing behind the scenes. King George the Sixth had taken on a young equerry, a former fighter ace who had distinguished himself in the war. A temporary engagement to begin with, the arrangement soon became permanent. Marrying in a romantic impulse, this equerry had not been able to put down deeper roots and the marriage had foundered. In 1947, the equerry had accompanied the Royal Family to South Africa and it was on this tour that a firm friendship developed between Group Captain Townsend and the King's younger daughter, then rising seventeen. In 1950, not even suspecting the warmth of his daughter's feelings, the King raised his equerry to the position of Deputy Master of the Household.

At the end of 1951 the King had become extremely unwell. An X-Ray showed a growth on the lung. An operation was performed but the doctor had told the Queen privately that the King might not live more than two years. Recovering well, the King pre-recorded his Christmas message, motoring to Royal Lodge Windsor, the home he most enjoyed. Just before Christmas he moved to Sandringham for the family festival. Princess Elizabeth and Prince Philip had just enjoyed an exceptionally successful tour of Canada and America. President Truman had said, "Like 1939, the tour of their delightful parents over again!"

Towards the end of January, the King was well enough to take his family to see 'South Pacific' at Drury Lane Theatre. The following morning he stood on the tarmac waving away his elder daughter and her consort on the first leg of their journey to Australia. They were due to spend a few days in Kenya.

On Tuesday, 5th February, 1952, the King was said to have taken a countryman's magazine to bed early, with the words to his wife and younger daughter, "I'll see you in the morning." Some time in the small hours of the 6th February, his life ebbed away.

I hope you are not growing too tired of all these descriptions. With the young Queen came another turning point in the nation's history, a new Elizabethan Age.

Queen Elizabeth's new life started at once. History discloses that black mourning clothes had been included in her luggage. The telephone calls and royal civilities completed, the Queen, accompanied by the Duke of Edinburgh, left the Kenya Treetops Hotel preparing to face the 4,000 mile journey back to London Airport. Awaiting her were three famous statesmen, the Prime Minister, Mr Churchill, the Leader of the Opposition, Mr Attlee, and the Foreign Secretary, Mr Anthony Eden. Standing next to them was the Queen's uncle, the Duke of Gloucester. It was dusk on a bitterly cold February evening.

Eighty-five-year old Queen Mary, awaiting the new Queen at Marlborough House, is reported to have said, "Her old Grannie and loyal subject must be allowed to be the first to kiss her hand." Privy Councillors gathered to do obeisance at the Accession Council. Harold Macmillan remarked, "Don't we all look shabby in our Ration Book clothes!"

Many thousands of mourners stood in the bitter wind queueing to walk past the catafalque where the late King lay in state in Westminster Hall. Queen Mary felt unable to attend the funeral but the late King's brother, the Duke of Windsor, arrived from Paris to join the funeral cortège. Queen Mary appeared to sense that she might not be present at her granddaughter's Coronation ceremony, leaving instructions that there should be no mourning for an ex-Queen Consort which might spoil the nation's Coronation rejoicing. In fact, when her time came in March 1953, her wishes were observed.

In Parliament, rising to the occasion as he always did, Winston Churchill proclaimed, "I, whose youth was passed in the august, unchallenged and tranquil glare of the Victorian era, may well feel a thrill in invoking once more the prayer and anthem 'God save the Queen'."

The hope of collaborating to build a new world-wide era of peace was not materializing, but, much more interesting to the public, was the spread of television, and the pent-up demand, soon to be fulfilled for new cars, motor cycles, freezers, and electrical gadgets of many kinds. Mr Churchill had declared that the end of rationing was in sight. The golden era of the motion picture was not yet in decline, but would soon need to adjust to the new world of shrinking audiences as television spread right across the land from home to home, even to families inhabiting caravans. This was the age when young people were developing new fashions of their own, calypsos, skiffle groups, early rock music, young men dressed in the supposed fashion of King

"Teddy Boys" in 1955.

Edward the Seventh calling themselves Teddy boys, and dancing with girls wearing stiletto heels and wildly swirling skirts.

In the autumn of 1952 the American Presidential election had resulted in a great Republican victory for General Dwight Eisenhower of war-time fame. The former President Truman moved into private life, but he, like his illustrious predecessor Roosevelt, had left an imprint on history. The new President now declared that, in his view, the free world of America was failing in its duty to protect other parts of the free world from the encroachment of Communism. It was this concern that was to lead, in due course, to the establishment of a particular policy in Indo-China, an area formerly ruled by France, but now divided into Laos, Cambodia and Vietnam.

At the Conservative party Conference that same autumn, Mr Harold Macmillan was congratulated on reaching his target of building three hundred thousand houses, a fine achievement.

An unexpected happening now unfolding was the very large-scale non-white immigration from the West Indies congregating in inner city areas, still suffering from bomb damage and social deprivation. With their totally different customs and life styles it was understandable that there was some prejudice.

Russia had now announced a successful atomic explosion, while the U.S.A. was edging towards the appalling destructive power of a nuclear explosion. In China, the Communist party led by Mao-tse-tung and Chou En-lai had set up a Communist People's Republic bringing about a regeneration of that immense country.

In March 1953, Josef Stalin died; Nikita Khrushchev emerged as the new Russian leader. The Soviet Union were now said to have tested an extremely alarming weapon known as the hydrogen bomb. It was at this point that Mr Churchill suggested a Summit Conference "better jaw-jaw than war-war" he declaimed in his characteristic phrasing. But it was to be some time before the Foreign Secretary Sir Anthony Eden (who had inherited his father's baronetcy) achieved a great triumph of diplomacy setting up the Paris Agreement leading to a European Defence Committee of the Western Allies.

The inhabitants of Great Britain and indeed of the Commonwealth were much more interested in the coming Coronation of Queen Elizabeth the Second, arranged for 2nd June, 1953. This event seemed to lead to a sense of security in a fast-changing world. One of the anomalies of the British Constitution, puzzling to foreign visitors, was that of the Earl Marshal, himself descended from a long line of Roman Catholic Dukes, having the authority to organize a Protestant ceremony in the shrine of Anglicanism, Westminster Abbey. It seemed even stranger that this Duke of Norfolk, the sixteenth, held his ceremonial office not, as might have been expected, by appointment, but by inheritance. Foreign journalists described the Coronation as an Alice in Wonderland dream with 'pack-of-cards' uniforms and impossible titles like Lord Great Chamberlain, Master of the Horse, and Mistress of the Robes. "The British love these bizarre customs," they wrote, "stretching back, as they do, to pre-Norman Coronations all taking place in this same Westminster Abbey. The new young Queen has consented to wear the immensely heavy St Edward's crown made of solid gold, instead of the much lighter Imperial Crown of State which had been made for her great-great-grandmother, Queen Victoria. The Imperial Crown of State is, we understand, the crown worn by British monarchs for the ceremony called 'The Opening of Parliament'. Readers might be interested to know that St Edward's crown was made for King Charles the Second, in 1661, to replace the original crown of St Edward the Confessor, a British king, which had been pillaged at the time of the British Civil War. It was said that all the Crown jewels were confiscated by Oliver Cromwell, the Lord Protector, following the execution of King Charles the First. The Orb represents the whole world subject to Christianity; the Sceptre with the Cross represents mercy, power and justice; and the Dove, of course, peace."

For the first time in history, television enabled millions to share in the Queen's Coronation Day, both inside and outside the Abbey, watching the Archbishop of Canterbury, Dr Fisher, (later Lord Fisher of Lambeth) and sharing the excitement of the thousands packing the streets; admiring the extravagantly gilded state coaches; the colourful Sovereign's escort of household cavalry with all their brilliantly clothed postillions and outriders, faithfully reported. "An overwhelming triumph of spectacle," announced the gifted B.B.C. Commentator whose voice had been at the background of the Abbey ceremony. It was Mr Richard Dimbleby too who, later in the day, described the gold flood-lighting, picking out the flowers, flags, bunting and pillars, massive lions and unicorns and towering poles, in the blues, scarlets, mauves and yellows for the benefit of the millions of listeners overseas. No one minded the rain. Television in 1953 was in black and white.

Visitors flocked to see an Agatha Christie thriller 'The Mousetrap' which was eventually to become famous as the longest run in the British theatre, far outstripping Oscar Asche's famous 'Chu Chin Chow' which ran from 1916-1922.

A week or two before the Coronation, the Queen had invited Mr Churchill, who had long declined an Earldom, to accept the honour of Knight of the Garter, enabling him to remain a member of the House of Commons. Sir Winston, as he now became, happily consented.

A much less happy episode, following the Coronation, now turned on the Queen's younger sister, Princess Margaret, who had declared her love for Group Captain Townsend maintaining that the couple wished to marry. The Queen declined to coerce her sister one way or the other, but the Group Captain, now Comptroller of the Queen Mother's household, was a divorced man with two sons, and certainly did not possess the kind of birth qualifications hitherto expected of a royal husband. At the Prime Minister's suggestion, Peter Townsend was invited to choose a post outside the royal household, while Princess Margaret was urged to wait for two years until the celebration of her twenty-fifth birthday. The curiosity of the world's press, chasing after her with telephoto lenses, was soon to make her life intolerable. The former member of the King's royal household and the late King's younger daughter had become world-wide news. At length, when the couple met again after a gap of two years, the Berkshire estate of friends where they were staying was surrounded by reporters and photographers, some breaking through hedges or attempting to scale walls. It became necessary to bring in police dog teams to track down the intruders. The situation had run out of control. Soon it had reached crisis point. The Princess herself brought it to an end by visiting the Archbishop of Canterbury renouncing her intention of marriage. There was much sympathy for her, many people feeling that a young woman's private life had been blighted. Some five years later the Princess married an agreeable young man, to be ennobled as Lord Snowdon, and the couple became the parents of two children. Sadly, the marriage was to go adrift and to end in divorce. A pleasanter future awaited the Group Captain to whom fate had been kinder.

By 1954, Sir Winston Churchill was approaching his eightieth birthday and his health was failing. The mainstays of his Conservative administration were Sir Anthony Eden, who had been the heir-apparent for some time, Mr R. A. Butler and Mr Harold Macmillian. Increasingly Eden was now assuming a larger share of control. Wages had increased sharply leading to a rise in the general standard of living. The grim years of austerity and shortages were passing at last. In the Labour opposition a feud had broken out between Gaitskell and Bevan. This was to reach a climax when Attlee left the House of Commons to accept an Earldom.

A four-power conference had been convened in Berlin in an attempt to settle the East-West differences over Germany, but the conference achieved nothing. The Russians would not agree to the holding of free elections leading to a possible re-unified Germany.

In the autumn of 1954, the Foreign Secretary, Sir Anthony Eden, succeeded in pulling off what was thought to be his most celebrated diplomatic coup by bringing together the representatives of nine countries to sign the nine-power agreement at Lancaster House. The countries concerned were France, Germany, Italy, Belgium, the Netherlands, and Luxembourg, together with Great Britain, Canada and the U.S.A. This agreement established a permanent basis of Western defence, bringing to an end the occupation of West Germany by the Western Allies. It was also to bring Germany and Italy, the two former enemies, into N.A.T.O. In addition, Canada and the U.S.A. reaffirmed their commitment of sending troops to Europe's defence.

The Soviet Union retaliated by bringing in the Warsaw Pact, an Eastern European mutual assistance treaty, concluded by Albania, Bulgaria, Czechoslovakia, East Germany, Poland, Hungary and Rumania. As lines of communication were no longer needed in Austria, that country was given her freedom.

As the weeks ran out at the end of 1954, Colonel Nasser took over the reins of power in Egypt. Brigadier Neguib had forced the abdication of King Farouk setting up a republic. Nasser, strongly anti-British, had secured the withdrawal of British forces from their former base on the Suez Canal. Soon his great hope proved to be the extension of Egyptian arable lands based on the building of a High Dam at Aswan.

In April 1955, Sir Winston Churchill, the grand 'Old Warrior' as he was now affectionately called, having passed his eightieth birthday, bowed out of politics. Under the new Prime Minister, Sir Anthony Eden, the Conservative party seemed geared to win the next General Election, called for May, which was won on the political promise of 'a property-owning democracy' the first step towards the rapidly increasing 'affluent society'. Political correspondents reported, "The vacuum of Labour opposition has been filled with nothing but the

Sir Anthony Eden (right) and Mr Harold Macmillan.

warring factions of noise. A group of Left-wing M.P.s have surrounded the party by strife." Mr Attlee's move to the House of Lords had left the Labour party in a state of turmoil. The Bevanites, as they were called, constantly voted against the party line, making clear their determination to nationalize as many industries as possible.

A round of strikes involving printers, miners, dockers and footplatemen did nothing to improve Labour's prospects. This spring election of 1955 was an easy win for the Conservatives. The Liberal Party's share of the poll, ever since the days of the 1930s National Government had remained insignificant.

The Daily Telegraph commented, "Few British Prime Ministers can have entered office regarded more as international statesmen than as mere politicians. Long training, knowledge and experience are indeed Sir Anthony's assets. In foreign affairs he is an acknowledged expert."

Good fortune for the new Prime Minister was destined to be brief. Mr Harold Macmillan, the new Chancellor of the Exchequer, shifted the emphasis on to saving, also introducing the novelty of premium bonds. But there were innumerable industrial stoppages while relations between employers and trade unions were worsening.

Overseas affairs were far from smooth. Terrorist activity had broken out in Cyprus, where the Governor had declared a state of emergency, and tribal nationalism was spreading in Kenya. Britain's resolve to remain in control led to unpopular measures of repression denounced in America as well as in the Soviet Union.

As the Prime Minister had stated, "The divisions of Europe and the 'Iron Curtain' have to be accepted as problems we must learn to live with. We must now turn our attention to the grave problems of the Middle East."

As the British troops had moved from the Suez Canal, Soviet influence had crept into Egypt. There were many reports that Russian trade with Egypt had increased and that Communist states had offered assistance with the building of the High Dam at Aswan, which Colonel Nasser believed would irrigate thousands of dry acres, thus adding greatly to Egypt's wealth and influence.

Russian help, however, did not materialize, causing Nasser to turn for help to the Western Powers. At the end of 1955, America had offered a loan of fifty-six million dollars, with the British adding a rather less generous loan. It was generally believed that American generosity was largely given to block the Communist liaison between

Russia and Egypt. Without warning, the American State Department abruptly withdrew the offer obliging the British to do the same. Nasser retaliated by announcing the nationalization of the Suez Canal Company. Eden became obsessed with the image of Nasser as a second Hitler threatening the whole fabric of Western security. "He has his thumb on our windpipe," declared the Premier.

Now followed the disastrous episode known as the 'Suez Crisis'. The shares of the Suez Canal Company were mainly held by the British Government and by French investors. Claiming that he only wanted the Canal dues because he had been let down by the Americans and British without reason, Nasser made clear that the canal would be blocked by shipping and made unusable if the money from the World Bank were not forthcoming. It transpired that the U.S. Senate had become thoroughly alarmed by Nasser's brand of international politics. Canal shipping now became trapped.

The Prime Minister was forced to come up with some kind of an answer to the complicated diplomatic problem. Losing control of the canal represented the end of British influence in both Africa and Asia. To a friend he said, uncharacteristically, as he was a man of peace, "It would be better to see Britain go down against Egypt with all flags flying than submit to this malicious monster." In America, General Eisenhower running for re-election as President, on a peace platform, was most reluctant to become involved in any military adventure likely to prejudice his chance of being elected for a second term, accordingly he advised the Secretary of State, Foster Dulles, to work for a compromise solution.

Eden felt that he had been strung along, and then let down by Dulles.

Meanwhile, military co-operation between France and Israel had reached a state of intimacy enabling the two countries, both for quite different reasons, to co-ordinate their actions. France had long equipped the Israeli armed forces to withstand an Arab attack. The French Prime Minister, Guy Mollet, succeeded in bringing the British Prime Minister to align Britain with the French-Israeli plans. On 29th October, 1956, Israel began operations against Egypt. Two days later, British and French planes attacked Egyptian bases and joint airborne forces landed at Port Said. American pressure at once forced a cease-fire to be arranged. Eden's reputation was destroyed.

The action of the British, French and Israeli forces was almost universally condemned. In mitigation it was being said that the Prime

Minister, a sick and exhausted man, had overestimated the need to control the Canal.

Feeling betrayed by the Allies, with only a short time to go before his presidential election, President Eisenhower approached the General Assembly of the United Nations who voted for a U.N. force to occupy the Canal Zone. Meanwhile, the combatants withdrew.

The International Monetary Fund stepped in to support the run on the pound sterling.

The now ageing Sir Winston, magnanimous as ever, remarked, "When a man is ill, his mind becomes tortured. He wanted to create peace in the Middle East but he nearly jeopardized the peace of the world." Others were less kind. "It was a blunder of immense proportions," said colleagues and opponents alike. The Suez expedition had divided the country, as well as the Conservative party, in two bitter opposing factions.

With the Anglo-American alliance threatened, undermining the foundation of post-war international relations, the Soviet Union took the chance of crushing an uprising in Hungary. A newspaper correspondent wrote, "The Suez affair has robbed the West of any moral advantage over Communism. Both are now resorting to force to secure their political objectives." For the first time, the British were compelled to face the fact that Britain was no longer a Great Power. Many new weak countries were emerging to become known as 'The Third World'.

One of the most unfortunate outcomes, not stressed at the time, was the collapse of the recently revived 'entente' between Britain and France. It was thought that one of the few positive results of Suez was disillusion with the burdens of Empire, shouldered by the British for so long. Perhaps the time was ripe, after all, to pursue thoughts of decolonization. By Christmas, broken in health, Sir Anthony Eden resigned. Later he was to accept an Earldom as the Earl of Avon.

Two obviously outstanding candidates were now available to take over the office of Prime Minister, R. A. Butler, and Harold Macmillan. In the event, the Queen was to send for Mr Macmillan.

If this was a time of a very troubled national conscience, the new Prime Minister revived the country's spirits. A colleague wrote of him, "A man of old-fashioned integrity, hard working, efficient, shrewd, straight as a plank, but with a deeply sympathetic nature. He should be able to shake hands with the nation's heart." It was the new Premier's task to try and make the country forget Suez. Buoyant and optimistic he quickly established his authority. Expansion without inflation had become his aim. Half-American himself, he soon set about restoring the old trans-Atlantic relationship.

In March 1957, Eisenhower and Dulles met Macmillan and Selwyn Lloyd, the new Foreign Secretary, at Bermuda. In due course, the two leaders were to sign a 'Declaration of Common Purpose'.

R. A. Butler had become Home Secretary and Leader of the House of Commons, while Peter Thorneycroft became Chancellor of the Exchequer. The new Prime Minister wished to place high value on material success and comfort, while remaining humanitarian.

Millions of pounds were now being spent on cars, motor cycles, lawn mowers, caravans, television sets, washing machines, freezers, even boats. Wages had risen sharply and this period was known as the real beginning of the 'affluent society'. Large sums spent on gambling, horse racing, drink, tobacco and entertainment were also rocketing. But there were to be many miscalculations, leading to pay pauses and credit squeezes which became extremely unpopular. The months ebbed on.

In this letter to you, my small namesake, I can do no more than write a sketchy account of the great historical events of the twentieth century. By the time you are of an age to be interested, the reports will all be available for inspection in the Public Records Office, should you find them worth perusing.

Meanwhile, as the southbound swallows were on their way in the autumn of 1957, the Independent Televison was making great strides and there was a craze for 'Bingo'. In giving thought to longer-term economic planning the Chancellor was meeting with uncooperative reactions from the T.U.C.

Self-government was now being speeded up in wide areas of Africa.

Rising income levels were now enabling young people to earn wages undreamt of by their fathers or grandfathers. For the young, active and mobile, life had become an exciting adventure. Thousands were not born at the time of Hitler's bombs. As has been the case with so many new rising generations, the young set themselves in opposition to all forms of authority.

For their parents, life was also changing. The generous wage packet enabled wives to make use of convenience frozen foods, carrying a transistor radio, to remove the boredom of housework, often squeezed in hurriedly before the chief 'breadwinner' came home, as wives, too, were now working. The expansion of car ownership had accelerated at an unexpected speed, long before the expensive road-widening schemes and new motorways could keep up with the need. When the first stretch of M1 was opened it was referred to as 'environmental vandalism!' As traffic congestion grew worse, many cities were to grieve at the hideous jungle of motorways and ugly high-rise buildings modern development was bringing in its train. As railway connections disappeared, domestic air travel doubled. Soon a great gulf began to open up between the older generation and the young.

Probably the greatest cultural revolution at this time was to be seen in the transformation of music. Pop music, as it was called, became a vast commercial enterprise. It started by expressing a massive protest against established society, to be bound up some time later with the development of electronics. Films and plays, representing the trend of rebellion against the country's life-style were soon drawing enthusiastic audiences. Possibly, as a result of this rebellion, vandalism and excessive mindless violence began to be taken up by the nation's youth, often expressed in rampaging football fans. Many felt that this new spirit of liveliness was good, but others were less certain. Some years later, it was to lead to an increasingly unstable, disorderly and violent society.

The early days of 1958 produced swords of ice and a great plane of snow. In France, the European Common Market, set in motion by the Treaty of Rome and signed by France, Germany, Italy and the Benelux countries, had now become a reality. This market was to cover the exchange of industrial goods, but more stress was to be laid on agricultural produce. Britain, with her system of Commonwealth preferences, did not place much significance on the Common Market.

General Charles de Gaulle had now returned to power in France. The great leader of the Free French forces distrusted the British, convinced that they were tied to the U.S.A. Few in Britain, at the time took much notice of these developments. Later in the year, to relax East-West tensions, Macmillan decided to visit Russia. A European Free Trade area was now negotiated, with the Prime Minister receiving praise for his record in Foreign affairs. He had also handled difficult Commonwealth affairs with tact and patience. In Home affairs, business confidence appeared to be steady and the country still seemed to be enjoying largely full employment.

It was thus with an air of optimism that holiday makers returned to work when summer had passed its peak. The fruitful earth seemed to be awaiting the ebb that would bring the first changing leaves, the red-rose berries of the yew, and the scarlet holly berries. Taking advantage of the lull, the Prime Minister called for a General Election which was to take place in October 1959.

Television had now come into its own as an election medium. Macmillan's political gifts, with a certain amount of theatricality, helped the Conservatives to win a decisive victory with a majority of over one hundred, a personal triumph for him after the despondency and grief which had followed 'Suez'.

The Labour party were still in disarray. Hugh Gaitskell, the new leader, supported Britain's need to remain in N.A.T.O. and to hold nuclear weapons, while the Left-Wing maintained that the total renunciation of the nuclear bomb would win moral leadership throughout the world.

As the first year of the 1960s ripened with the greening of spring, and the fragrant blossoming of wayside flowers, the tide of changing public taste became much more noticeable. There was a sharp retreat from the social controls of Victorianism.

Four young men from Liverpool, sporting a different hairstyle, and with a dashing new exuberant image formed a Pop culture which was to reach a peak of success beyond imagining. Their songs were tuneful, but they were soon to be followed by others with a much wilder anti-establishment message. In a very short period, any collection of young people, with, or without talent, provided they could pay for the equipment, could set themselves up as Pop Groups, or Pop musicians. This was to lead to a whole decade of change. Cannabis was soon to become the characteristic drug of the new youth culture. Restraints were abandoned. "Do your own thing!" became the call of the young. All the old forces of law and order seemed to be breaking down.

Fashions became drastically changed. Long hair for men had become a fashion emphasis, while both sexes wore T-shirts, often carrying messages, and blue denim 'jeans'. The name had originated in Genoa just after the war when denim boiler suits, suitable for builders, were the only available new clothing for the one-time extremely impoverished Italians.

Groups of 'Hippies' or Flower Children as they called themselves with their motto 'Make Love not War' proliferated like some

The "Beatles" together again.

uncontrollable spreading weed. Young men were soon wearing
talismans, charm bracelets, necklaces, even earrings. Young women
starting a different fashion, wore long trailing skirts with tangled
unkempt hair. Both sexes (to the horror of their parents) joined together
in Squats—a name given to derelict, unoccupied properties awaiting
bull-dozing.

   In addition to the young drifters and lay-abouts, as their elders called
them, better educated young people, given great opportunities by the
opening of a wide variety of new Universities, refused to conform.
Sweeping aside old values, they participated in demonstrations, sit-ins,
marches, rebellion and vandalism.

Distressed tax payers watched them sadly. "These are the élite," it was being said, "the new beneficiaries of the welfare state, chosen to be the spearhead of the country's progress. If authority is to be sapped from the inside, no wonder we are seeing a surging increase in crime!" A relaxation in public decency was beginning to emerge.

Mr Harold Macmillan's admirable political talents had earned him the name of 'Super-Mac'. As the 1960s advanced, however, the magic appeared to be fading. Treasury predictions were beginning to go awry leading to a deficit in the Balance of Payments. For the first time since the war the British found themselves encountering severe competition from other countries in the world's markets. Steps to hold down wages ran into serious conflict with the Trade Unions.

In America, the new Secretary of State, Dean Acheson, had declared, "The British have lost an Empire but have not yet found a rôle." Hopes of British nuclear independence, because of the intolerable cost, had faded, leaving the British largely dependent on the U.S.A. This dependence was seized upon by General de Gaulle propelling him to block British hopes of entering the European Common Market.

The sudden emergence of a new young Democratic American President John F. Kennedy, in the autumn of 1960, caught the world's attention. He was soon to achieve spectacular success in Foreign affairs. Many regarded his election as a symbol of hope and inspiration.

By now there was a warm understanding between West Germany and France. Both countries suspected that the Anglo-American special relationship would never benefit Europe. De Gaulle continued to veto British entry making his famous speech to the British, "You people who eat the cheap wheat of Canada, the succulent lamb of New Zealand, the potatoes of Ireland, the butter, fruit and vegetables of both Australia and New Zealand, and the sugar of Jamaica, would never want to buy the agricultural produce of France which would cost you more." The nation's interest remained muted.

Meanwhile, Mr Edward Heath, the energetic and prominent member of the Conservative party who had been given special responsibility for European affairs commented, "We shall continue to work with all our friends in Europe for the true strength and unity of the Continent."

The years of 1961 and 1962 ran their course. The population was growing richer. It was not only business men, but Pop singers, film stars, fashion photographers, models, T.V. stars, football players, and boxers who were pushing their way into the world of very high earnings. Hire-purchase flourished. Thousands now owned cars.

In the autumn of 1962, President Kennedy had scored a brilliant success in what was known as the 'Cuban Missiles Crisis'. Aerial photographs had convinced the President that ballistic missiles with atomic warheads were being installed by Russia in America's close neighbour, Cuba. The request to Khrushchev to arrange for the removal of these missiles led to the reply that Russian missiles would be removed from the island provided that all N.A.T.O. missiles were immediately withdrawn from Turkey. This condition was at once rejected by Kennedy. A crisis ensued. Kennedy stated that the U.S. Navy would impose a blockade on Cuba. There was now a grave risk of nuclear war. A week later, Khrushchev agreed to withdraw the missiles under United Nations supervision, on the understanding that America would lift the blockade, at the same time, giving an assurance that Cuba would not be invaded by U.S. forces.

The naval blockade ended with a Soviet pledge to withdraw all bombers, missiles and rocket personnel which were subsequently

President John F. Kennedy on his visit to Ireland, June 1963.

dismantled. Kennedy's firmness in this crisis greatly enhanced his prestige as a statesman both at home and abroad.

In British affairs, all over the once flourishing Empire, decolonization was proceeding. Independence had been granted to Nigeria, Cyprus, Sierra Leone, Tanganyika, Jamaica, Trinidad, Uganda, Kenya, Zambia, Zanzibar, Malawi and Malta. Some parts of the one-time Commonwealth were soon to choose entirely different names.

As 1963 flowed on, after a winter of almost Siberian severity, it became evident, for the first time since the Hitler-war, that the high demand for labour was falling. The dreadful qualms had appeared again that many citizens might find themselves unemployed. Automation was often responsible, but the trend widened, speeding up the sudden decline in the Government's prestige and popularity. The B.B.C. was allowing public figures to be mercilessly lampooned in satirical programmes, adding to the general deterioration in public standards.

Soon after the Labour leader, Hugh Gaitskell, had died, in the spring of 1963 still in conflict with the Labour Left-wingers over nationalization and unilateral nuclear disarmament, Harold Wilson took over the leadership. It was therefore Wilson who was to taunt the Conservative Prime Minister about the relationship between a certain call-girl and the Conservative War Minister. The episode seemed to touch on national security as the same call-girl had allegedly entered into an association with a Soviet Naval Attaché. The Minister denied impropriety but later admitted that he had misled the House, resigning from office.

Harold Macmillan's popularity was said by certain newspapers "to have taken a nose-dive". The relentless publicity given to the subsequent revelations, including a doctor's suicide, seriously damaged the Government's standing. It became clear that the private lives of some very distinguished people were far from pleasant. The rumbustious Lord Hailsham blurted out on a television interview that, in his view, adultery was not restricted to members of the Conservative party, or even to the rich! Macmillan, a man of impeccable moral rectitude had had no knowledge whatever of these activities. In common with many others, he lamented the serious decline in public standards. The backwash, however, seemed to flow over his Government.

Having worked unflaggingly since the Suez crisis of 1957, the

Premier's health was suffering. At the beginning of October 1963 he was rushed to hospital for an operation. Expecting to be away from politics for some weeks, the Premier resigned from the leadership, instructing the Foreign Secretary, Lord Home, to undertake the processes whereby a new Conservative Prime Minister would emerge. This decision was taken on the eve of the Conservative Party annual conference, creating a huge political stir at Blackpool.

After a widespread 'behind-the-scenes' struggle, with three outstanding candidates, Lord Hailsham (who had undertaken to renounce his peerage) R. A. Butler, and the recent Chancellor of the Exchequer, Reginald Maudling, party opinion began to swing behind the quiet and modest Foreign Secretary, Lord Home. He himself had never even considered putting himself forward as a possible candidate. When the Queen visited the bed-ridden former Premier in hospital, he recommended that she should summon Lord Home to Buckingham Palace.

Fighting a by-election conveniently arranged for him in a Scottish constituency, the new Prime Minister entered the House of Commons at the beginning of November 1963 as Sir Alec Douglas Home. A charming man; but his aristocratic orgin and lack of experience of Front Bench politics enabled the brilliant leader of the Opposition to represent him as a person completely out of touch with the modern world. The Labour party, at last sensing victory at the polls, closed ranks behind Wilson their new leader.

Sir Alec, gifted in the Foreign Office, did not prove to be a sparkling parliamentary debater, despite boisterous Conservative support.

On 22nd November, the world was deeply shocked to hear the news that President John Kennedy had been assassinated while driving in a motorcade into Dallas. The perpetrator of the outrage was said to be a man named Lee Harvey Oswald, who was himself shot at point-blank range while under police custody, two days later. The grief and disillusionment of this young President's death extended far beyond the shores of the United States. His successor, President Lyndon Johnson, was later to face the mounting unrest when the North Vietnamese in attempting to win the South were repulsed by massive military intervention of U.S.A. forces. Hostility between the two armies was to continue for many years. The angry outcry in the U.S.A. eventually destroyed the President's health, forcing him to seek retirement.

Britain was now rapidly changing. Of the many outstanding

personalities who had become famous by the mid-century, such as Glyndebourne composers, musician, poets, writers, novelists, painters, architects, sculptors, athletes, B.B.C. announcers, and Television interviewers, it is rash to hazard a guess, but probably the best remembered will be the 'angry young men' dramatists who completely changed the style of the theatre. In place of the comfortable escapist plays of the 'between the wars' era, there now developed a strong Left-wing-slanted agitational type of play, known as 'kitchen-sink drama'. The first of these, 'Look back in anger' was written by John Osborne, soon to be followed by John Mortimer, Arnold Wesker, Harold Pinter, Shelagh Delaney, Peter Shaffer, and Ted Willis. A number of new experimental theatres opened. New actors included Michael Caine, Peter O'Toole, Albert Finney, Tom Courtenay, Anna Massey, Glenda Jackson, Judi Dench, and Dorothy Tutin. There were many more. The young followed their own Pop-culture. With generous wage-packets they spent their money on transistor radios, musical instruments, long-playing records, motor scooters, and way-out clothes. This was the time of strip-tease clubs, one-armed bandits, drugs, drink, gambling, and the deafening noise of juke-box music. Many young people formed themselves into rival gangs breaking into vicious fights. The antagonists gave themselves special names, Mods, Rockers, Hell's Angels, travelling long distances to engage in a savage battle, often on Bank Holidays.

There were more exciting happenings. The jet engine had been produced, also the hovercraft, and it was the time of the early micro-chip revolution. In Russia, the pioneer Soviet cosmonaut, Yuri Gagarin, had become the first man to travel in space, completing an orbit of the earth in the satellite of the Vostok spaceship. In America, Commander Alan Shepard had penetrated space by over a hundred miles. There was soon to be an acute rivalry in the developing space race between these two great Powers.

The population of Britain was thought to have achieved a better standard of living than ever before. Much had been accomplished— better housing, longer holidays, holidays with pay, shorter working hours, more foreign travel, vast ownership of cars, television, washing machines, freezers, and a much wider opportunity for every kind of recreation and leisure. The redistribution of wealth had become much more even. Powerful Trade Union leaders were beginning to assert their economic strength, the strike weapon being used more frequently, not always to industry's advantage.

The paper-back book revolution was putting good books within the reach of many, affording unprecedented opportunity for personal study. Domestic staff had now virtually disappeared leading to great changes in kitchen gadgetry such as washing-up machines. Laundrettes, coin operated, where the family wash could be carried out and spun dry, had become popular, proving to be convenient meeting places.

It should be noted, however, that the Conservative government had paid little attention to the new challenge being posed by Germany and Japan. So much more energy had been devoted to improving conditions in the British Isles. It became realised too late that not enough money had been channelled into key industries.

In the autumn of 1964 Sir Alec Douglas Home called for a dissolution of parliament and the country entered into one more confused and characteristic hubbub of a General Election.

Harold Wilson, a very forward-looking egalitarian gave a virtuoso television and platform performance, winning an overall majority of four seats. Meanwhile, strikes were increasing alarmingly in growing resistance to any kind of governmental policy regarding wage restraint. The new Labour Government's next two years were to be dominated by the economy.

I am sorry there is so much repetition in the story of these years. You will be growing very tired of politics. There were much the same crises—economic difficulties, mini-budgets, recalcitrant trade unions; but Wilson created a new Department of Economic Affairs under the explosive leadership of Mr George Brown. A less noisy Minister, James Callaghan, was given charge of the Exchequer. Also joining the Cabinet came a fiery left-winger, Barbara Castle, to head a new Ministry of Overseas Development. Harold Wilson was now offering a 'New Deal'. It was soon to run into trouble.

The Cabinet weathered a dangerous sterling crisis and then set about the creation of a 'Prices and Incomes Policy' signed by representatives of the Government, Industry and Trade Unions.

Meanwhile, on 25th January, 1965, the great war leader, Sir Winston Churchill died. His life had spanned ninety years including a place in history which few could attain. All over the world, obituary tributes appeared, mountains of flowers were sent to Lady Churchill. Day and night, for the last fortnight of his illness crowds had stood silently outside his London home. Operation Hope-Not, which he himself had organised for his funeral, began to move. It was said to be the last State funeral for any commoner. Across the world, flags flew at half-mast, lights were dimmed, and in London, theatres closed, while Parliament adjourned. He was to lie in state in Westminster Hall, the only Prime Minister to do so since Gladstone. Several hundred thousand queued in the roads outside, in the falling sleet, to pass by the catafalque. The scene was pictured by television and recounted by radio. The funeral service at St Paul's Cathedral proved to be one of the great public ceremonies of history. Rarely could so many kings, queens, princes, presidents, prime ministers or Service Chiefs have assembled to do honour to this unique man. "A symbol of indomitable courage" was the world's opinion. He was laid to rest at Bladen, Oxfordshire, next to his parents, and less than a mile from his birthplace, Blenheim.

After yet another General Election the autumn of 1966 saw Harold Wilson's government with a much bigger majority. The Prime Minister was also to see himself faced with the intractable attitude of Mr Ian Smith, who had achieved a landslide victory against decolonization of White Rhodesia. Ian Smith declared a Unilateral Declaration of Independence. Wilson, finding himself compelled to satisfy the angry African clamour for help, sought the application of immediate economic sanctions.

Sir Alec Douglas Home had returned to the House of Lords pressing the Conservatives to undertake a new procedure for electing a leader. Instead of the many private consultations which had existed formerly, there was now to be a vote inside the parliamentary party. The party chose Edward Heath, a man of marked contrast to Earl Home. An amateur musician of some ability, Mr Heath's lively debating skill and continued work for Europe were now to be rewarded.

The Liberal leader, Jo Grimond, had resigned having been replaced by an energetic younger candidate, Jeremy Thorpe. The Liberals still remained very much a third party.

Trade Union strength was becoming unassailable. Greatly adding to Wilson's economic difficulties there had been a strike of the National Union of Seamen causing a paralysis of the docks, a great loss of exports, and a corresponding weakening of the pound sterling. After much anguished argument the Cabinet were faced with devaluation or deflation, finally deciding to deflate with the announcement of a wage freeze.

There were many other threats in these worrying times, pollution, DDT, chemical fertilizers, antibiotics, crop sprays, broiler-reared chickens, the contraceptive birth (or anti-birth) pill, new plastic materials which could not be destroyed. The spoilation of the green countryside went clattering on.

Material wealth was certainly proving to have its adverse side. The Government's wage freeze, followed by severe restraint, ran into great trouble with the Trade Unions. By mid-summer 1967, the country's gold reserves were falling. Wilson relaxed hire-purchase controls to stimulate a consumer boom. The Trade Unions answered by pushing for wage increases.

An Arab-Israeli war of June added to the difficulties by closing the Suez Canal and vastly increasing the nation's trade deficit. By the autumn, the need for devaluation had become paramount. A sudden dock strike called in both London and Liverpool did little to help. With some personal courage, well aware of the Government's growing unpopularity, Wilson devalued the pound sterling making his well known statement, "This does not mean that the pound in your pocket has been devalued." This gave Edward Heath the chance to reply, "Three years of Labour Government has reduced Britain from a prosperous nation into an international pauper!"

The Chancellor, James Callaghan, defended devaluation with dignity, but agreed to resign, moving over to the Home Office, while Roy Jenkins took his place.

The incidence of continuing strikes urged the Prime Minister to consider a total reform of industrial relations. The outcome was to be a White Paper called 'In place of Strife' with fines in the event of non-compliance. Many Labour members felt that the whole foundation of the Labour party had depended upon the unions, who were in fact their paymasters. A great outcry arose against the plan. The pugnacious Employment Secretary, Barbara Castle, desperate for Trade Union reform, struggled against the opposition, only giving way, at length, when there was a major Labour back-bench revolt. The T.U.C. answered, "Compulsory legislation and statutory financial penalties against unions will never regulate strikes." The Labour Cabinet capitulated.

February 1960 had seen the birth of a second son to the Queen and the Duke of Edinburgh, followed, four years later, by a third son.

When the Queen was on one of her many overseas tours, at the time of John Kennedy's Presidency, a rumour circulated that an impertinent American press-woman had asked the Queen, "Why don't you wear dazzling fashion-conscious clothes like Jackie Kennedy or Grace Kelly?" The Queen is reported to have given the courteous reply, "I leave that to my sister." Rather less controlled was the forceful Duke of Edinburgh who bounded forward, "Don't you dare put that camera in the Queen's face." "You are very prickly!" retorted the journalist. A French magazine wrote, "When Queen Elizabeth the Second rides along the Mall, the Duke, her Consort, and her eldest son and heir, at her side, the Household Cavalry massed behind her, she is an annual focus for affection, pride and loyalty. If ever the British want her to leave, an overwhelming welcome will be found in France!"

Of all the problems inherited by the British, none would have been more readily discarded than the seemingly eternal sectarian strife in Ulster. In 1968, Richard Nixon had become the new President of the U.S.A. largely as a result of the unpopularity of the Democrats deeply involved in the exceptionally divisive campaign of running the Vietnam war. Nixon's arrival coincided with a world-wide ascendancy of civil rights movements, often pressed by students with riotous and questionable behaviour. This tendency had spread to Northern Ireland. The Northern Ireland Civil Rights Association, consisting largely of Roman Catholics, a minority in Ulster, began to agitate for full equality with the majority community. A civil rights march from Belfast to Londonderry in January 1969 was broken up by police, fearful of disturbances. This was quickly followed by widespread rioting, extreme violence and many acts of arson and sabotage. The old sectarian rift began to widen.

In August 1969, following the annual march of the Protestant 'Apprentice Boys' the Catholic population of Londonderry barricaded themselves into a section of the city set up as 'Free Derry'. Serious riots followed with many injured. James Callaghan, the British Home Secretary, ordered the British army to be moved into Londonderry and Belfast to separate the warring factions.

Once again, British politicians found themselves caught up with the impossible mission of satisfying the opposing factions in Ulster. Loud and clear sounded the old voices of militant Irish nationalism. An I.R.A. Army council, self-elected, split off from the Officials calling themselves 'Provisionals' or 'Provos'. These 'Provos' then began a campaign of urban terrorism. An intensification of street violence was to lead to imprisonment without trial. This measure provoked more violence breaking out in bombings and shootings. The problems of the province grew steadily more serious. Bomb outrages were to spread to Britain.

A more breathtaking event was taking place on the other side of the Atlantic when the Apollo II Moonship was launched from a Saturn rocket at Cape Kennedy. It landed on the moon enabling Neil Armstrong and Edwin Aldrin to walk on the moon's surface. Neil Armstrong spoke the famous words, "A small step for man, a giant leap for mankind."

These American moon missions were to continue for six years linking up in 1975 with the Soviet Soyuz 19 Spaceship, when Russian and American crews exchanged visits. The mounting expense finally put an end to the Apollo project.

It was at this moment that Mr Richard Crossman, a member of Mr Harold Wilson's earlier Cabinet, published his diaries. They made sour reading with their story of gossip and intrigue. The story of the country's economic inadequacy ran in tandem with the legacy of the affluent sixties—the ferment of protest and disillusion, pollution, strikes, permissiveness, and the razzmatazz of rebellious youth.

The 'swinging sixties' had almost run their course.

The country was soon to approach a much more solemn decade. With no statutory incomes policy, and no compensating curbs on the trade unions, Britain was about to enter a period of union turmoil. As weekly wage rates and average earnings were pressed higher and higher, frequently accompanied by strikes, there was no comparable growth in productivity. This soon brought about an acceleration of inflation. At the same time, the Labour Government's deflationary policy had led to mounting unemployment. It was soon evident that the increasing cost of importing raw materials would oblige manufacturers to lay off staff.

Even so, the trend still seemed to be running in Labour's favour, accentuated by favourable gains in the spring Borough election contests, accordingly Wilson took the chance of calling for a General Election in June. To the surprise of many, it was the Conservative party, led by their recently elected leader Edward Heath, who were the victors, gaining an overall majority of thirty seats. Heath had been able to announce with perfect truth, "The Labour economic policy produced lower growth, higher unemployment, and faster rising inflation than when the Conservatives left office in 1964." To the public, there seemed little to choose!

In June 1970, when Heath took up the reins of government, he was to find himself facing the same problems.

As General Charles de Gaulle had now died, Heath made a determined effort to revive the possibility of British entry into the European Economic Community which had lain dormant. The new Conservative Prime Minister remained convinced that Britain's economic future rested with Europe. A strong, clever and purposeful man, Iain Macleod was appointed Chancellor of the Exchequer. His unexpected death, a short time later, was to prove an irreparable loss. A young woman politician, hitherto not well known, Margaret Thatcher, was appointed Minister for Education and Science.

It was a fresh government, but all the same apparently insoluble difficulties were to continue, mounting inflation, the alarming situation in Ireland, increasing unemployment, the stagnant economy, the attempt to curb public expenditure, the control, far too late, of the ever-increasing pressure of coloured immigrants, the struggle to limit wage increases. It gave the impression of an old gramophone record with the needle stuck in the same groove. The same problems remained depressingly constant, regardless of who resided in 10 Downing Street.

Mr Reginald Maudling, a keen Home Secretary, felt compelled to resign because of a business association with an architect charged with corruption. Anthony Barber, who took over the Exchequer, never acquired his predecessor's authority.

Seeking desperately to limit wage increases by means of a gradual reduction of pay settlements in the public sector and thus reduce inflation, the Government met with furious resistance on the part of the trade unions. The National Union of Mineworkers were soon to smash their way through the government's guidelines by picketing power stations. Holding the country to ransom they secured a wage increase of thirty per cent.

Once again trade union power was brought to the forefront of the Cabinet's thinking and a new Industrial Relations Bill was worked out. The unions simply boycotted the Bill which reached a flash-point when five dockers' shop-stewards were on the point of being committed to prison for refusing to obey. They were released at the last moment by the House of Lords who set aside the judgment. Having determined to be 'martyrs' the five exploded with fury deeming the House of Lords to have taken a 'diabolical liberty!' The new Act only succeeded in making industrial relations worse. Meanwhile, a phenomenal rise in world commodity prices, chiefly oil, was beginning to take place.

The Yom Kippur war between the Arab states and Israel in October

1973 led to the quadrupling of oil prices. This forced Mr Anthony Barber to announce wide cuts in public expenditure, a surtax surcharge and great restrictions on hire purchase. Miners, power engineers and train drivers began an overtime ban.

Mr Heath's great achievement of getting Britain into the Common Market earlier in the year, and his shock treatment of Northern Ireland introducing direct rule from London, to provide a breathing space, were now eclipsed by the action being taken by the trade unions. The oil price rise had put the miners in a very strong position. Seeking to pacify them, Heath offered more money to cover 'unsocial hours'. The concession did not satisfy them and the pressure on the power stations in mid-winter now forced the country into a three-day week. The nation's dwindling energy supplies were disappearing. After many more unsuccessful negotiations and faced with a darkening crisis of 'doomsday' proportions, the Government brought in a state of emergency. The N.U.M. answered with an all-out strike.

Giving way to mounting pressure from colleagues but against his own instinct Heath decided to seek the country's mandate—Who rules, democratically elected government, or trade unions?

An election was called for the end of February 1974, bringing Harold Wilson back to Downing Street. The miners were given what they wanted.

A political commentator wrote, "Heath had tried to bring the country into a new age, but the antagonisms built up prevented the public from giving him the support he deserved. He has been unlucky, he should have won. The increase in world commodity prices, and the tragic events in Ulster, distracting so much attention, were quite beyond his control."

The first bachelor Prime Minister since the younger Pitt, without even a home of his own, Edward Heath departed leaving his supporters distressed and confused. Television viewers watched with some sympathy as the former Premier's treasured piano was loaded on to a removal van outside No 10. Despite the often synthetic enmity shown on the Front Benches in parliament, a certain amount of chivalry existed. Harold Wilson at once offered Heath the sanctuary of Chequers, should he have no immediate home, but an old friend stepped in offering a London flat. Caught again by the television cameras, Heath's dejected expression revealed a cruel insight into a man's private disappointment.

Mr Edward Heath.

Sir Harold Wilson.

The late Harry Truman's words were remembered, "If you can't stand the heat, get out of the kitchen!"

A foreign commentator wrote, "Are the Trade Unions the root cause of British national decline? Their excessive wage demands with no corresponding increase in productivity and their refusal to consider all forms of technological progress are bound to keep inflation rising."

Harold Wilson's new government with his wafer-thin majority was soon to meet with the same depressingly familiar problems. Every move the Conservatives had made to try to pacify the Irish had fallen down like a pack of cards. The men of violence on both sides continued to be completely irreconcilable.

If Ireland could not be appeased, Wilson could at least ease the trade union confrontation. Bringing in an unwritten Social Contract he hoped for a period of industrial peace. This was not to be realized. By the summer there was widespread dislocation on the railways, constant trouble in the motor industry and growing militancy among hospital workers. Denis Healey, the new Chancellor, added to the country's gloom by announcing large increases in the cost of coal, electricity, steel, and a steep rise in the cost of postage stamps and rail fares. A danger of a serious recession was now imminent.

Probably the Labour Premier's most intractable problem at this time still remained Rhodesia. Ian Smith had now declared Rhodesia a Republic. There had been personal meetings between Harold Wilson and Ian Smith on board H.M.S. *Tiger* and later on board H.M.S. *Fearless*. Both meetings had broken up in failure. Internal warfare in Rhodesia was to continue, only to be settled eventually when Ian Smith at last consented to take a more sympathetic line towards his black colleagues. Independence for the new Zimbabwe, under Robert Mugabe, at last enabled Britain to escape the worrying responsibility as a result of negotiations in a London all-party Conference, signed eventually in 1980. In the meantime guerrilla wars continued. Concern was expressed in the reduction of status for the whites.

In America, President Richard Nixon, elected for a second term, was striving desperately to reduce American involvement in the increasingly unpopular Vietnam war. His Secretary of State, Henry Kissinger, known as a peripatetic ambassador, enabled Nixon to improve diplomatic contacts with China which was to lead to a cease-fire in Vietnam after the President's personal visit to Peking. Nixon's record was destroyed by what became known as the Watergate scandal, when it was proved that the President had connived in the illegal practice of withdrawing information from the secret files of his political opponents. Pressure against him rose so sharply that he resigned in August 1974, his place being taken by his Vice-President, Gerald Ford. Scandal also surrounded Nixon involving his previous Vice-President, Spiro Agnew, who had become embroiled in a less than straightforward financial deal.

In home politics, there had been a considerable rise in the votes cast, not only for the Liberal party, but for the Scottish and Welsh nationalists. The Liberals, who had declined Heath's offer of supporting a Conservative administration after the February 1974 election, now attempted to foster a realignment with Labour. It proved of little value. In the election of October 1974, it was the Scottish Nationalists who were to make the most significant advance. Another party, now increasing its tally of candidates but not of votes was the National Front.

The result produced a Labour win with a majority of about thirty. The battle of the economy was far from won. Average earnings greatly increased while productivity remained static.

The Social Contract with the Trade Unions was not working as Wilson had hoped. Denis Healey's new budget in the spring of 1975 was, as he expressed it himself, rough and tough.

Soon there was another crisis of confidence in the pound sterling and Healey had to ask for help from, the International Monetary Fund.

The compulsory wages policy, attempting to reduce the rate of inflation, together with a strict price code was soon to bring about a frightening increase in unemployment. Then followed the Government's apparent inability to contain the Public Sector Borrowing Requirement.

Probably the only happy factor was the success of the North Sea oil fields, leading to the establishment of a new British National Oil Corporation. The country had almost forgotten good news!

Through these worrying years, the Conservatives, unhappy with a leader who had lost two consecutive electoral campaigns, began to consider the possibility of a replacement. It was generally supposed that Mr William Whitelaw, affectionately known as Willie by Government and Opposition alike, would be most likely to emerge as Heath's successor. After a round of ballots, the new means chosen by the Conservatives, the result was a surprise, Margaret Thatcher had been elected with a clear majority, the first woman leader to be chosen by any major political party.

Soon a number of Conservative by-election victories raised morale. If Edward Heath felt despondent a commentator wrote a line of praise, "His success in carrying out immensely difficult negotiations for taking Britain into the European Common Market, after the long months of failure, because of French obstruction, should ensure him an honoured place in our turbulent twentieth century story."

Back in 1968, a brilliant Conservative politician, and former Cabinet Minister, Enoch Powell, had made known his desire to check the rising growth of coloured populations flowing into Britain. He had predicted racial conflict on an immense scale. It had now become necessary to appoint a Race Relations Commission and it seemed as if the traditional British social cohesion was breaking down. In the new economic gloom, particularly among the young, groups of white teenagers with shaved heads, calling themselves punks and skinheads, began to form gangs. Like the young blacks, they had started to fight a sullen civil war with authority. These young people, unlike the protesting 1960s students, were largely at the bottom of the educational scale.

By mid 1976, Jeremy Thorpe's luckless association with a so-called male model had led to his resignation, allowing his successor, David Steel, to take over the Liberal party leadership. Meanwhile, Harold Wilson produced a shock resignation just after the celebration of his sixtieth birthday handing over the Labour leadership to James Callaghan. If Wilson had secret reasons for his unexpected departure, they were never disclosed. The Queen offered Mr Wilson the Order of the Garter enabling him to retain his seat in parliament, becoming Sir Harold. An enigmatic Prime Minister, it was thought that Wilson would certainly leave his stamp on these troubled years.

Thirty years had now passed since the advent of Mr Attlee's first Labour Government following the end of the Hitler-war. A whole new generation had grown up who had never heard of Belsen, Buchenwald, Auschwitz, Dachau, Ravensbrück and other merciless and brutal German Concentration Camps, run by the Nazis, where millions were murdered by overwork, starvation and the gas chamber. Still less were they aware of the German Führer himself, as the British and American bombs smashed down, degenerated into a broken, raving figure, in a concrete shelter, far below the ruins of the Reich Chancellery. Time had moved on.

Perhaps one of the greatest achievements since 1945 had been the establishment of the National Health Service.

The rise in living standards was perhaps the central phenomenon of the three decades. Consumerism, the growth of Supermarkets, hire-purchase, and afterwards credit cards, had led to a change of life-style beyond imagining in the early days of the century.

In resource and development there had been many successes, scientific and technological innovations, computers, tape recorders, video cassettes, colour television, instant communication by satellite, record players. Some acts of parliament, too, were to have an irreversible influence—the Abortion Act, the lowering of the voting age to eighteen, the joining of the European Economic Community, the Immigration Act, Comprehensive Schooling, Law and Order, to say nothing of the innumerable acts relating to Social Security, unemployment and sickness benefits. If there was joy in "Women's Lib" and permissiveness, it had an adverse side in the number of deserted wives and unmarried school girl pregnancies. Single parent families were the first to fall into poverty. The "road-to-freedom" had also led to militancy, violence and terrorism, I.R.A., bomb outrages, and a great increase in the horrible crime of hi-jacking aircraft holding passengers to ransom. Also a steadily increasing proportion of the population are now becoming old.

This last happening may well produce a mounting political problem for your generation, little cousin, but now I must take you along to the end of my letter, if you have been able to bear with me so far. Mr Callaghan's Labour Government struggled on. Any solution to the problem of Northern Ireland seemed as remote as ever.

As Labour began to lose by-elections, the new Premier made a working pact with the Liberal party. David Steel made clear that this represented a move towards possible future deals in a 'hung' parliament. The arrangement gave Callaghan time which was to enable the economy to improve slightly.

In the Chancellor's budget of April 1976, increasing pensions and Family Income Supplement, Mr Healey produced a package of tax cuts conditional upon a Trade Union agreement limiting pay increases to three per cent. His device met with mixed reaction. Price controls were maintained, with a vigorous campaign in favour of cuts in public expenditure, now mounting substantially. Interest rates were raised to a high level but not enough to prevent another dramatic slide in the pound sterling. Once again, the Government was forced to seek a loan from the International Monetary Fund.

In 1977, the dollar became weak and the pound rose. By 1978, small signs in economic recovery were apparent, but there were now nearly two million people unemployed. It seemed impossible to win.

Many bills inherited from the Wilson era were now passed, perhaps the most noteworthy being the abolition of selection in secondary education, known as the 'Eleven-plus', together with a new Race Relations Act creating a new Commission for racial equality. There was also a Devolution Bill granting separate referendum elections in both Scotland and Wales. The Dock work regulation bill gave registered dockers a job for life, even with the right to stand and watch others working, while drawing their pay. "A crazy trammel on economic progress!" said the Conservatives.

Many had begun to feel that the generosity of the Welfare State had become too lavish. Would it not be wiser to concentrate more on supporting industry, the nation's actual 'breadwinner', it was being asked.

The currency, which had now been decimalized on the basis of one hundred new pence to a pound, losing the old familiar penny, shilling, florin and half-crown and introducing 10p and 50p coins, made purchases appear much more expensive. Soon the traditional English weights and measures were beginning to give way to grammes, and metres. In the schools, the old subjects like Latin had begun to be replaced by Social studies. Formal teaching methods were being challenged. There was renewed concern about literacy and numeracy. The comprehensive educational system, while possibly succeeding in social egalitarianism, was certainly failing to produce educated citizens.

Capital punishment, suspended first for five years, had now been abolished. Crime, particularly juvenile crime had soared. Women criminal offenders had also risen.

The immense rise in rates had driven many businesses to move from city areas, leaving behind derelict inner cities. The disturbing feature of this was the growing friction between young blacks, who had assembled in these run-down areas, and the police. Ugly rioting followed.

At the opening of 1979, the Labour Government fixed a target rate of wage increases at five per cent, a figure the trade unions were to call 'derisory' stressing their determination to achieve double the rate, more if they could attain it. This led to widespread industrial dislocation which became known as 'The winter of discontent'.

Mrs Margaret Thatcher in the 1979 election campaign.

A dangerous strike by firemen was followed by lorry drivers, hospital workers, ambulance men, dustmen, sewage workers, and even grave diggers, all pressing home their claim of higher wages. The much vaunted Social Contract had turned out to be nothing more than a hollow sham. The grave diggers' strike in particular caused deep public outrage.

In the general election which followed in the spring of 1979, public disgust turned against the Labour Government. Voters were now clamouring for legal curbs to be made against trade union power. The result was a Conservative victory, which, for the time in British history was to bring a woman Prime Minister, Margaret Thatcher, into 10 Downing Street.

Rarely had a new Premier been faced with more exacting demands, except in war. There was tension between East and West, the two great powers of Soviet Russia and the U.S.A.; starvation in Asia and Africa; Third world debts; rising interest rates; the threat of the interruption of oil supplies; terrorism in Ireland; inflation, homelessness, drug-taking, crime, and rising unemployment. Would the new Prime Minister meet the challenge of the future?

As a well-known theatre critic was wont to write, "Never judge in haste, the last Act crowns the play."

This seems a fitting stage for the conclusion of my letter to you my youthful, two-year-old namesake. I hope it has not bored you. History has no chapters, no curtainfall, the world goes spinning on. The twentieth century has seen the world change from horse-drawn vehicles to lunar travel. There have been catastrophic wars, but great social, economic and scientific revolutions. As we approach a new century, the spirit of man and woman will go striding on.

Midsummer 1984 has bloomed. Outside my window, pink-tinged clouds dip into a luminous sea. Lights begin to gleam. The birds are still singing sweetly in the evening sunshine. Twilight deepens. Tomorrow, yet another birthday dawns for me. I am now an old-timer, not likely to be around when you celebrate your coming-of-age in the year 2000. I hope I may be hovering in the shadows watching you cut your cake. Perhaps you will hear me whisper, "May all your ventures prosper, and may the shining new 21st Century enfold you in kindly arms."

Bibliography

The World Crisis, Winston S. Churchill.

The History of the Second World War, Winston S. Churchill.

Our Times, Stephen King-Hall.

George the Fifth, Arthur Bryant.

Diaries of Sir Henry Channon.

Diaries of Harold Nicolson.

Edward the Eighth, Frances Donaldson.

Roosevelt, John Gunther.

Old Men Forget, Lord Norwich.

The Man who created Hitler, Viktor Reimann.

David Lloyd George, John Grigg.

Ernest Bevin, Mark Stephens.